Beyond the Main
Coastal British Columbia Stories

Copyright © 2015 Wayne J. Lutz

All rights reserved. No part of this publication may be reproduced, stored in a retrieval system, or transmitted, in any form or by any means, electronic, mechanical, photocopying, recording, or otherwise, without the written prior permission of the author. Reviewers are authorized to quote short passages within a book review, as permitted under the United States Copyright Act of 1976.

Note for Librarians: a catalog record for this book that includes Dewey Decimal Classification and U.S. Library of Congress numbers is available from the Library and Archives of Canada. The complete catalog record can be obtained from their online database at:
www.collectionscanada.ca/amicus/index-e.html

ISBN 978-1-927438-18-3
Printed in the United States of America

Powell River Books
Powell RIver, BC

Book sales online at:
www.powellriverbooks.com
phone: 604-483-1704
email: wlutz@mtsac.edu

10 9 8 7 6 5 4 3 2 1

Beyond the Main
Coastal British Columbia Stories

Wayne J. Lutz

2015
Powell River Books

To Fred...

A fellow of integrity who lives on an island
And helped me realize my fondest dreams

Front Cover Photo:
   Looking down on Powell Lake from Heather Main
Back Cover Photos:
   Windsor Lake near Goat Lake Main

Books by Wayne J. Lutz

Coastal British Columbia Stories
Up the Lake
Up the Main
Up the Winter Trail
Up the Strait
Up the Airway
Farther Up the Lake
Farther Up the Main
Farther Up the Strait
Cabin Number 5
Off the Grid
Beyond the Main
Up the Inlet
Powell Lake by Barge and Quad
Islands and Inlets

Science Fiction Titles
Echo of a Distant Planet
Inbound to Earth
Across the Gallactic Sea
Anomaly at Fortune Lake
When Galaxies Collide

Pacific Northwest Series
Paddling the Pacific Northwest
Flying the Pacific Northwest

*The stories are true, and the characters are real.
Some details are adjusted to protect the guilty.
All of the mistakes rest solidly with the author.*

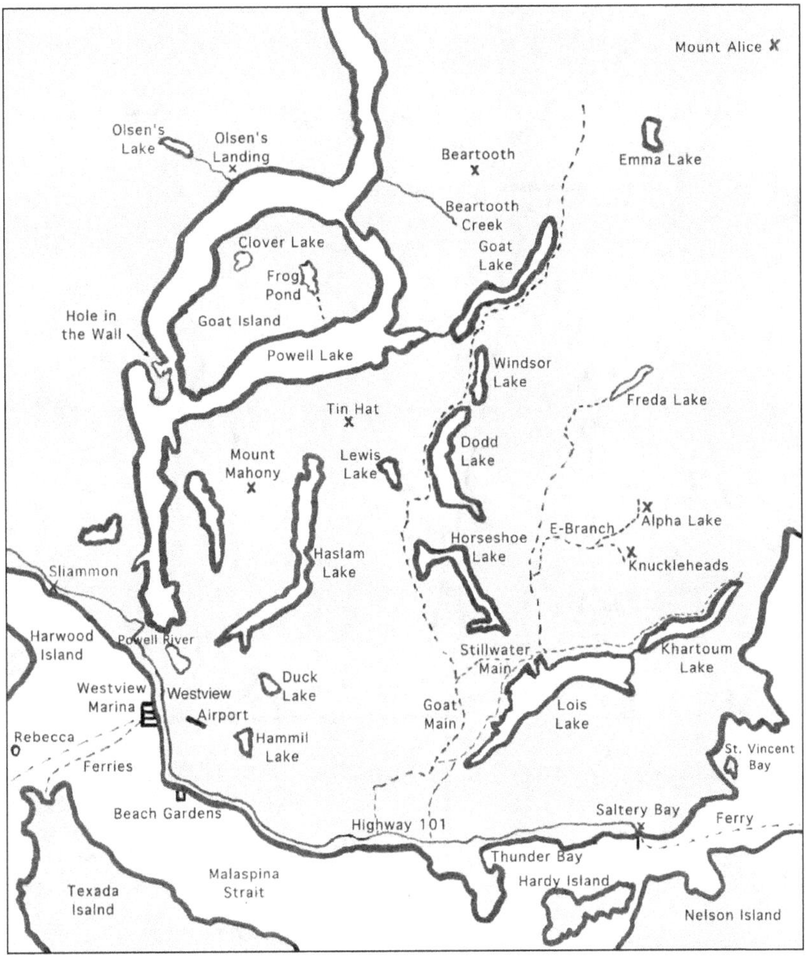

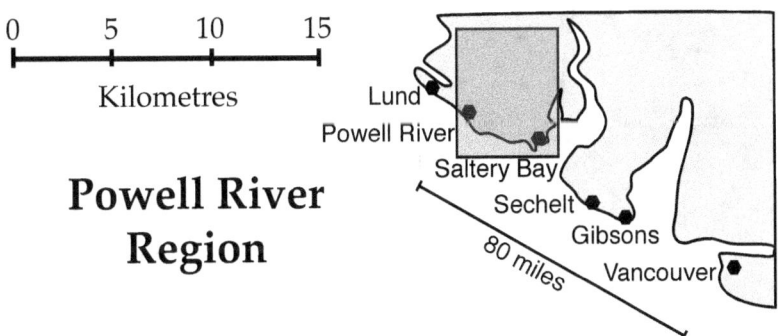

Powell River Region

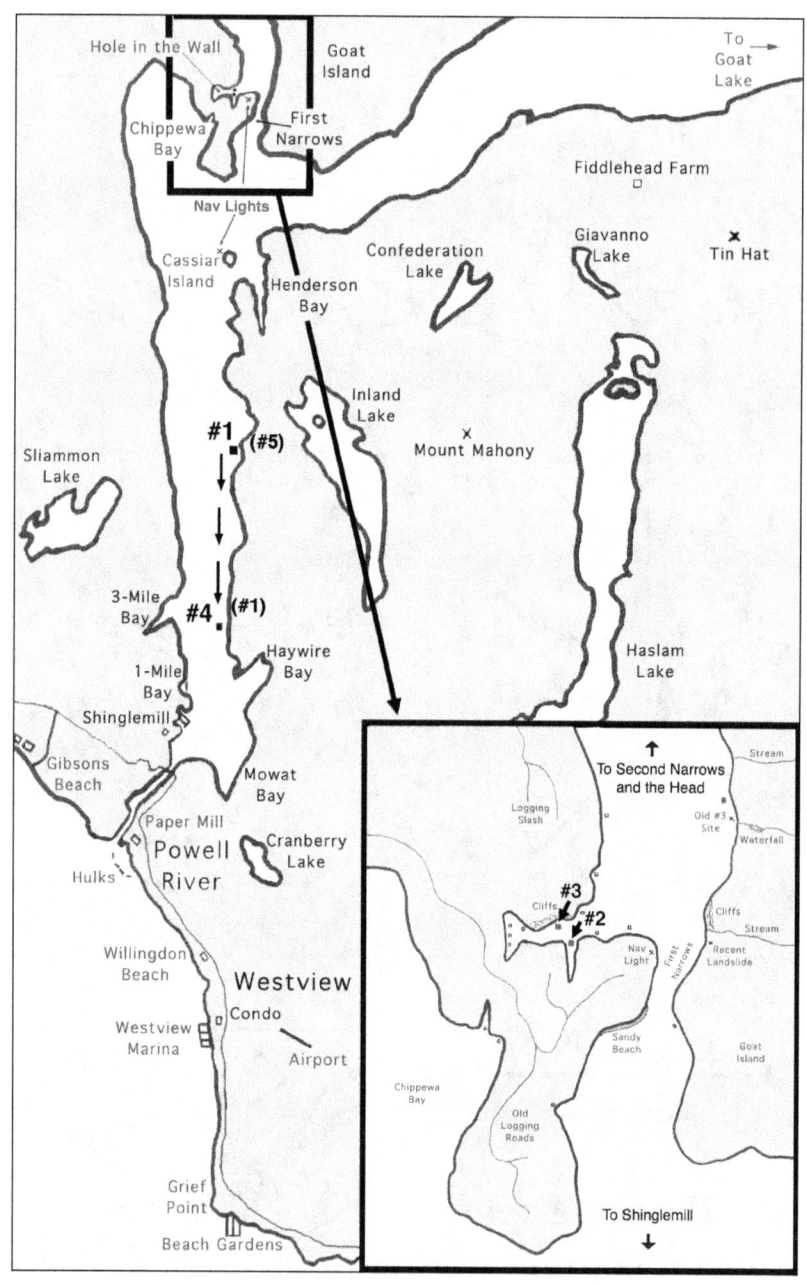

Lower Powell Lake

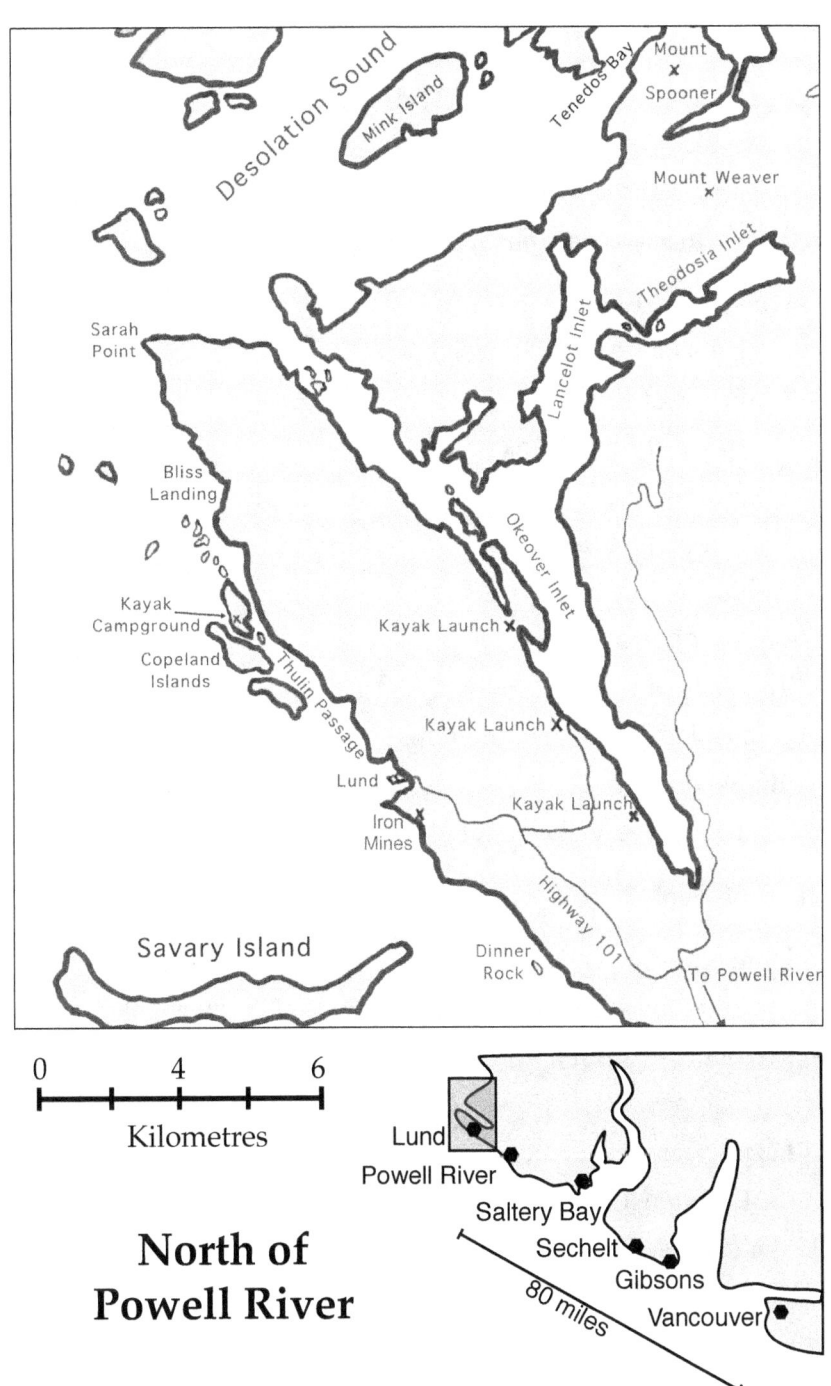

Contents

Preface – Quads – Multiple Scenarios 12

1 – Quads on a Raft 14
    Hole in the Wall, Powell Lake

2 – At the Head 27
    Head of Powell Lake

3 – Bear Siren 49
    Head of Powell Lake

4 – Following Logging Trucks 63
    Theodosia Valley

5 – The Edge of the Wilderness 70
    Haslam and Giovanno Lake

6 – The Wednesday Crew 80
    Theodosia Valley; Elk Lake

Center-of-Book Photos 96

7 – Home Base 99
    Theodosia Valley and Hole in the Wall, Powell Lake

8 – Mechanic without a Toolbox 109
    Chippewa Bay, Powell Lake

9 – Lake Dreams 127
    Chippewa Bay, Powell Lake

10 – Lake Barge 140
    Saltery Bay and Powell Lake

Contents

11 – Goat 155
    Goat Island, Powell Lake BC
12 – Narrows Main 163
    Narrows Dock, Powell Lake BC
13 – Olsen's 175
    Olsen's Landing, Theodosia River

Geographic Index 189

About the Author 191

Preface

Two Quads – Multiple Scenarios

When the first edition of *Up the Main* was published in 2005, the chapters were developed from my experiences riding off-road with my friend, John. He introduced me to ATVs, and soon Margy and I were departing regularly on rides from the Powell River Airport hangar, where our quad trailer was stored.

In 2012, we moved our bikes to Hole in the Wall on Powell Lake, a spot we thought would be temporary for the summer. But keeping our quads at the Hole year-round solved a problem we faced in all seasons. When we're at home in our cabin, we're hesitant to leave. When it's good weather for riding quads, it's also good weather on the lake, so leaving Hole in the Wall to trek to the airport and then the backcountry was difficult. Plus, the hangar storage location incorporated plenty of obstacles to slow us down – breakfast in town, confront the Internet, talk to Wally and Bob at the airport, to say nothing of the basic process of accessing our equipment. Quite often, especially during off-season months with shorter days, travel up and down the lake forced us to stay overnight in town for the sake of an off-road ride. Both a day and a night on the lake had to be sacrificed for a quad ride, a rather unacceptable situation.

But keeping our quads at the Hole introduced new limitations. There's only one road out, leading to Chippewa Bay. From there we could explore Museum Main or climb the mountain trail to Heather Main. But the ride to connect with other logging roads and trails is a long one, including the roads leading to Theodosia Valley or Olsen's Landing. Although getting to our quads from our cabin was quick, the riding days could still be long, and we had limited destinations. Meanwhile, most of our friends ride in the Goat Main region to the east of Powell Lake, and almost no one we know rides in the Chippewa Bay area, so we missed their companionship. The Powell River ATV Club bases their operations to the east of Powell Lake, and we had no connection to this region via Chippewa's logging roads.

Then an eye-opening event unlocked some new possibilities. Travelling to the head of Powell Lake with John, slowly pushing a cedar log raft loaded with our quads and camping gear, I discovered a region wide open for exploration. Besides this memorable trip to the Head, there are plenty of interesting logging company docks and barge ramps elsewhere on the lake, although the raft was a rather inefficient mode of transportation. Instead, imagine hopping aboard a pre-loaded landing craft moored at my cabin, and heading out for a quick day-trip or an overnight camping adventure. This would even give us access to the Goat Main system of roads and trails where the ATV Club rides, using barge ramps at nearby Fiddlehead Farm and further east on Goat Lake.

So in 2014, we began looking for a landing craft to solve our one-trail-out dilemma in Hole in the Wall. If we owned a landing craft, based at our cabin, we could keep our quads on the vessel, allowing a quick departure for barge ramps anywhere on Powell or Goat Lake.

Thus, our home haven for quad adventures has evolved over time. First came the town-based airport hangar, with its cumbersome scenario for accessing the mountains. Then the move to Hole in the Wall and a quick taste of Powell Lake via raft. Finally, the ultimate means of carrying our quads – a landing craft – an idea that took an unexpected deviation along the way with the purchase of a self-propelled barge. This book spans these changing modes of off-road exploration, which goes to prove – quads can enter your life innocently, and grow spontaneously and elaborately from there.

Wayne J. Lutz
Powell Lake, BC
March 31, 2015

◊ ◊ ◊ ◊ ◊ ◊

Chapter 1

Quads on a Raft
Hole in the Wall, Powell Lake

At 9 am, I pull into Hole in the Wall, towing my firewood raft behind the Campion, with two fishing lines still deployed after a trolling-speed tow north from John's Cabin Number 5 (the same site as his original Cabin Number 1). I stop outside the breakwater to retrieve my lures. The first yellow daredevil comes in fine, but the second snags when the rooster-tail hook catches the long towline leading back to the raft. I give up on the lure for now, and concentrate on shortening the towline by hand-pulling the raft towards the Campion. Once the rope is short enough, I'll be able to easily navigate through the breakwater entrance, and I can unhook the errant lure after I'm parked.

Once inside the boom, I hop out of the Campion and onto the firewood raft, and tie it to one of the big breakwater logs. While I'm on the raft, I manage to free my trout lure from the towline.

Everything is now in place for later today, when John will arrive to work on two projects requiring the raft – installation of a new cabin cable at Cabin Number 2 (across the Hole) and replacement of a smaller boom cable at my cabin (called Number 3).

"John phoned," says Margy, as soon as I reach the deck of the cabin. "He wants you to call him right away."

"When did he phone?" I ask.

"About 8 o'clock."

John almost never calls that early. On most mornings, he gets going slowly. This must be important.

When John answers my phone call, it's obvious his 8 am call arrived a little too late.

"I was trying to reach you before you brought the raft up to Hole in the Wall," he says. "I woke up this morning with an idea."

"What's the idea?" I ask.

"Well, I thought you should leave the raft at my lower cabin. Then we could tow it to the beach at the Shinglemill and load our quads on it. Wouldn't it be great to go up to the Head with them? We could leave the quads on the raft tonight, and head north tomorrow."

"It's a little late for that. The raft is already here. I suppose I could tow it all the way back down there after we're done with our projects, if you really want to go to the Head."

I've been to the head of Powell Lake with John on small 100cc motorcycles, and it was a lot of fun. The motorbikes fit on the 24-foot Bayliner's aft deck, and we had quite a ride. Imagine what we could do with quads.

"It was just an idea," says John. "I suppose we could still do it. I'm getting kinda' antsy to do something this summer."

It's not like John hasn't done anything exciting this summer, but he hasn't had a major overnight trip, something he usually does in the Bayliner, typically a trip to a remote area on the chuck. This summer, however, the Bayliner sits in the boat yard, awaiting major engine work, and the repairs have been delayed repeatedly by other projects in the shop.

John has traveled a long way on the chuck already this summer, but it was only a one-day trip in his 16-foot Hourston. On that journey with Eldon and Terry, he covered a lot of ground, all the way to Loughborough Inlet and back. It's the kind of trip I'd prefer to travel over the course of at least five days. Most people take weeks for such a trek, but John travels real fast.

His proposed trip to the Head with a towed raft will take 7 hours one-way, so it sounds like a three or four-day trip to me. It also sounds wonderfully appealing. I love it when I get John's full attention on a quad ride, with no other riders joining us – talk about a learning experience.

On the phone, we discuss what might have happened if his telephone call had gone through before I left to pickup the raft and bring it north. Could've done this, could've done that.

"The weather forecast looks good," says John. "Right through the weekend."

The weekend will be a busy one on the lake, a three-day August holiday for almost everyone, with BC Day on Monday.

"Imagine how busy it'll be at the Shinglemill this weekend," I say.

The Shinglemill and Mowat Bay are the boat launch ramps on Powell Lake, both just outside of town, and they're busy locations on holiday weekends.

It's already Friday, so I can't see any way to load two quads on a raft at Kinsman's Beach near the Shinglemill for the next few days. I don't like crowds. John hates them.

"Maybe we can load the quads on Saturday or Sunday," suggests John. "The big crowds will be going up the lake tonight, then back home on Monday."

"That's true," I reply. I pause, and then add: "Let's do it."

This probably surprises John. It's not because I'm opposed to doing stuff like this, but usually I cry bloody murder when anyone tries to pry me away from my floating cabin in good weather. But we've just experienced three straight weeks of nearly perfect conditions, so I'm willing to give in a bit for the sake of an adventure like this.

"Okay!" exclaims John. "We'll figure it out. I'll come up later today so we can get those jobs done with the raft. Then we'll decide when we can load our quads."

* * * * *

THAT AFTERNOON, JOHN TOWS THE RAFT across the bay to Number 2 with his Hourston, while I follow behind in my tin boat. We're planning to tackle the installation of a new cable from the cabin to shore, the connection stretching 200-feet underwater, from a corner of the cabin float to the base of a large tree. The old, frayed cable is still in place, holding the cabin in place for now, but we need to replace it with several hundred feet of new, seven-eighth-inch cable that weighs several hundred pounds. How we do this is a typical innovative twist of John's aquatic engineering abilities.

First we slide a long, thick rope under the brow log at one end of the raft, and then extend the rope over the cross-logs of our floating platform to the brow log at the other end, where it slides back underneath. Now the raft will ride freely beneath the rope. Then we stretch the ends of the long rope from the cabin corner all the way to the anchor tree on the far side of the bay. My tin boat serves as a good vehicle to get us to shore.

When the rope is secure on the tree, it'll temporarily hold the cabin in position as we replace the cable, and the raft will be our work platform. Next, John uses his gasoline-driven grinder to cut the old frayed cable at the tree connection.

With the tin boat tied to the raft, we pull it back to the cabin, sharing hand-over-hand tugs on the rope. We load the big coil of new cable on the raft, and head back to the anchor tree – again sharing tugs – with the tin boat once more towing the raft. John wraps one end of the new cable around the tree, using a shackled loop as the connection. We slowly pull ourselves back across the bay again, dropping cable as we go. Every few feet, John uses duct tape to connect the cable to the rope. This prevents the heavy cable from snagging on the bottom of the bay, and keeps the underwater portion shorter, which saves us from hauling an even bigger weight.

If laying 200 feet of thick cable across the bay sounds physically demanding, it is! If it sounds time-consuming, that's an understatement. But finally we install a new loop connection at the cabin's brow log, and pull ourselves back across the bay <u>again</u>, cutting the tape connections between the cable and the rope as we go. The cable droops to its natural position in the water, and the job is finally done.

There's still one more task for the raft, but it's a simpler one. We tow the raft back to Cabin Number 3 behind the tin boat, where we replace a much shorter cable connecting my breakwater boom to shore. This job is so straightforward that we could have done it with just the tin boat, but the raft makes the job quicker and easier.

By 5 o'clock, John is on his way back to town, with a farewell thought as he departs.

"Let's plan on loading the quads Sunday morning, before people show up to swim at Kinsman's Beach."

"Sure," I reply. "Give me a call when you decide what time."

"If you can tow the raft back to Hole in the Wall on Sunday, we'll plan to leave from there the next morning."

"Sounds good. Are you sure there won't be any logging activity at the Head?"

"Nah, nothing going on at all. We'll have the place to ourselves."

"Okay, let's do it!"

I'm sure John is still baffled by my complete lack of resistance to the major excursion he's planning in his ever-fertile mind.

* * * * *

AN HOUR LATER, while Margy and I are soaking in our private granite-rimmed natural swimming pool, the phone rings. If you don't get to the phone in five rings, it'll go to voicemail, so we don't even try.

Margy leaves the pool first, climbs up the wooden swim ladder onto the deck, and disappears into the cabin. A few minutes later, she's back.

"John left a voicemail. He says you should call him immediately."

"Immediately" sounds foreboding, like an emergency. The last time John left a message like this, our truck had been broken into at the Shinglemill. I dial him up right away.

"So is this immediate enough?" I ask.

John laughs, but then explains why he needed to talk to me so promptly. In his set of personal values, this really is a near-emergency.

"When I got back to the Shinglemill tonight, Terry was just leaving in his tug, pushing a big barge with a whole lot of people on it. Tents, a truck with a camper, and lots of other equipment, maybe even a few quads. I was too far away to see for sure whether there were any bikes, but I bet they're going up to the Head."

"Sounds like a holiday weekend outing," I say. "But maybe they're not going to the Head."

"No, I'm sure of it. Where else would they be going with all that stuff? They're gonna' ruin it for us. We don't want to be at the Head with a shitload of people."

"That wouldn't be fun. I wouldn't like it. You'd hate it."

"Watch for them. They should be going past your place in a few hours."

"Okay. Maybe I should go out in my tin boat and ask them where they're going."

John laughs, but I know he thinks it would be a good idea. I can't imagine my doing such a thing involving a moving barge.

When John hangs up, I think it through, discussing various scenarios with Margy. Maybe the barge isn't going to the Head. If it's a group of friends, they could be planning on spending the weekend on Goat Island, Chippewa Bay, or even Rainbow Lodge. The lodge has been closed as a commercial venture for many years, but who knows what a gang of partying folks might be planning to do.

Terry's tug, *River Yarder*, is one of the nicest on the lake. Did John say he was pushing the barge? That's rare, since tugs on this lake usually tow barges rather than push them. But if he's pushing, it would allow people to pass back and forth to the boat during the trip. Terry is probably taking advantage of this big recreational contract to enjoy the weekend himself.

"Let's go for a ride in the tin boat," I say to Margy.

"Okay. You don't want to just wait for the barge to pass?"

"If they turn for Chippewa or Goat Lake, we'll miss them. Let's go south and find them before they reach the North Sea."

* * * * *

WE GET READY TO GO, motoring out of Hole in the Wall promptly, and then south through First Narrows and out into the North Sea. From here, we can look north into Chippewa Bay, east towards Goat Lake, and all the way south towards the Shinglemill. There are a few boats zipping back and forth in the fading evening light, but no barge.

As slow as tugs go, I doubt they've reached here yet, so it seems likely the barge must still be to the south. I point our bow at Cassiar Island, and a few minutes later we see a big gray shape headed up the lake, currently near the Wash Out. We continue south to meet it.

What a night for a boat ride! The water is perfectly smooth, the sky clear and not yet fully dark, with a nearly-full moon rising in the east. Any excuse for a ride in a tin boat on an evening like this is a good one. And this time we have a mission.

As we approach the barge, I'm astounded at how full it is. There are several pickups, a truck with a big camper shell, a small excavator, and tents pitched everywhere in between. No quads to be seen, but an excavator!

We pass to the right of the oncoming barge, which is being pushed by *River Yarder*, and then cross behind the tug and a small boat that's being towed along. *Whomp! Whomp!* Two distinct thumps as we cross over the wake of the tug and its trailing boat, and then around to the other side and back north. On this side of the barge, there are two more boats attached, including a moderate-sized crew boat. This is one major outing!

Now we're rather close to the tug and barge, and almost as near to shore on our other side. I slow a bit, still considerably faster than the tug, and ease even closer to the barge to inspect its contents. The forward loading ramp is fully raised, and two guys are standing precariously on the platform extension. They wave, we wave, and then I add some power and pull ahead. From there, we head back to Hole in the Wall.

An hour later, Margy and I sit on our deck, waiting for the barge. Darkness has taken over now, and I figure it'll be quite a while until the slow vessel arrives. But in the background, I hear a powerful engine running at a fairly high power setting, and it's approaching from the south.

The barge appears, pushed by the *River Yarder* at what seems a frantic speed. I barely have time to inspect the barge with my binoculars before it disappears behind the granite cliff to the north. I've never seen a tug pushing so fast. Then again, if the guys aboard are paying for the fuel, why not? It's a long way to the Head.

It's time to file my report with John.

"An excavator!" he says. "Are you sure?"

"Yes, but it was a small one. What the heck are they going to do with an excavator?"

"Don't know, but wouldn't it be great to have one of those?"

"No quads aboard, though," I reply. "That's a good thing. It's getting too dark to follow them any farther," I report. "But I'll go farther up the lake in the morning to see if they stopped at the Clover Main dock or Olsen's Landing."

"They're going to the Head, quads or no quads." John replies. "I just know it. What a bummer."

* * * * *

THE NEXT MORNING, I take another ride in the tin boat. This time I travel up the lake to see if the barge stopped at Clover Dock or Olsen's Landing. If wave conditions permit, I'll even go as far as Rainbow

Lodge to check things out. North of there, all that's left is Beartooth and the Head.

The barge isn't to be found, although I don't make it all the way to Rainbow. The up-lake winds are building, typical of a summer day, and it becomes uncomfortable in the tin boat. After Clover Dock I cut across the lake's west side, where I can look all the way to Olsen's Landing. As far as I can tell, there's no sign of the barge in that area. Then I return to Hole in the Wall and file my telephone report with John.

"Let's hold off loading our quads until the barge returns," he says. "That will probably be Monday, at the end of the holiday. No sense going to the Head while they're around."

Coupled with a bit of unsettled weather now appearing on the long-range forecast, our whole plan may be out the window. At best, it looks like another week before we can get to the Head.

* * * * *

AT ABOUT NOON ON MONDAY, I hear the tug approaching from the north. In a few minutes, *River Yarder*, it's engine running slower now, passes by with its (in my imagination) load of tired passengers. No one is perched on the front landing ramps, and I don't see the excavator. But there's no doubt they're headed back to the Shinglemill. We'll be, hopefully, the next recreational explorers at the Head.

* * * * *

ALTHOUGH *RIVER YARDER* AND THE UPCOMING STORM have delayed us, we continue with our plans, getting as many things done in preparation as we can. On a regular trip to town for groceries, Margy and I hook up to the raft and tow it south to John's Cabin Number 5. Since it tows so slow, that's a significant step towards the eventual quad on-load at the Shinglemill.

Passing through First Narrows, Margy drives the boat while I perch myself in the bow, soaking in the sunshine and listening to the radio, with my fishing pole dragging a lure in a slow troll. The weather continues to be nearly perfect. The touted incoming storm is supposedly still inbound, but the weather remains superb – an August to be forever remembered – continuously clear, with calm water and

Margy towing the raft down the lake

warm (but not hot) temperatures each day for over three weeks in a row.

So now the raft is positioned at John's cabin, within 5 klicks of the Shinglemill and in a good location for John to make some final modifications. To get a little more speed out of the raft, he streamlines the front by cutting the logs below the waterline at a 45-degree angle. This should reduce some of the water resistance, while raising the front out of the water a bit for better performance.

I watch as John uses his chainsaw to cut the logs underwater. He positions himself over the front of the raft, with his chainsaw at an awkward angle. Since he's dressed in his normal summer attire, shorts and no shoes or socks, I can't help harassing him.

"So is this normal logger attire? Shorts and bare feet. Looks real safe."

He laughs, but acknowledges my next statement –"Be careful!" – with a sincere nod.

John prepares the raft

When he finishes the first cut, he stops and turns off the chainsaw before proceeding to the next log. I keep hounding him.

"Was the red stuff flying from your saw cedar chips or blood?"

* * * * *

BEFORE THE FORECAST STORM MOVES THROUGH, we use a sunny Thursday morning to load our quads onto the raft. It isn't a simple process. Logistically, it's the perfect project for John to coordinate, since he thrives on such complexity. The exercise will involve bringing the raft the rest of the way down the lake (a job assigned to me), using John's truck to load and unload two quads at the beach (necessitating two separate trips to town), getting both quads aboard the raft (properly secured), and bringing the raft back to Hole in the wall in preparation for our eventual departure.

In the first of these logistical steps, I hook the raft to the Campion at Cabin Number 5 at 7:30 am, to meet John at the Shinglemill beach (Kinsman's) at 9 o'clock. Meanwhile, John will go to the airport to pickup Margy's quad from the rear of our quad trailer (it's easier to use her quad, since it's loaded last-on and first-off), and then he'll meet me at the beach.

When I arrive at the Shinglemill, John isn't yet in sight, so I unhook the towline and drift a few hundred metres offshore from Kinsman's Beach, prepared to push the raft ashore. In just a few minutes, John arrives, with Margy's silver quad in his pickup bed. He motions to a wide-open spot on the shore.

"I'll push the raft in!" I yell to John.

"Sure. Just bring it in, whichever side is easiest."

We've discussed how we'll do the loading, so I orient the bow of my boat perpendicular to the side of the raft, and begin pushing. The beach is sloped enough that I can push the raft almost all the way to shore before it grounds in the gravel. There's still plenty of clearance for my engine, but I turn off the motor and raise the leg to be sure it doesn't hit bottom while we load the quads. Now I can go aboard the raft and help John.

With the edge of the raft still positioned a few metres offshore, grounded in shallow water, John off-loads the silver quad from his truck, and then slides the loading ramps out to me on the raft, where I position them for the wheels. In just a few minutes, John has the first quad up on the raft. We jostle it around a little for a bitter fit.

While John returns to his house to pick up the second quad, I use a hammer to install some log staples at locations that should work for both bikes. Using loading straps, I secure the silver quad, and have barely tied it down when John returns with his truck. This man is fast!

John's quad goes on just as flawlessly as the first, and within a few minutes the load is secure and ready to be pulled back into deeper water. I hook up the towline, and smoothly pull the loaded raft away from the beach. As I look back, John and his trusty Labrador Receiver, Bro, are disappearing in the distance. Both are staring at me, carefully supervising my technique.

The tow to Hole in the Wall is stable and relatively fast in almost perfectly calm water. All the way up the lake, boats approaching me head-on and overtaking me from behind pull in close to inspect the unique load, sometimes slowing as they approach to get a better look. You can't keep anything secret for very long on this lake.

Departing the Shinglemill

I'm able to tow comfortably at 1400 RPM, which gives me a GPS speed of 4.6 knots. Total time from Kinsman's Beach to Hole in the Wall is almost exactly two hours.

Raft positioned at Cabin Number 3

Now with the loaded raft docked at my Cabin Number 3, we're on the verge of departing for our big adventure. The forecast still shows a storm moving through over the next few days. But then we should be on our way.

Chapter 2

At the Head
Head of Powell Lake

JOHN IS INTENT ON PUSHING THE RAFT to the Head. I'm intent on making a test of both towing and pushing before we decide which is best. As usual, John wins, without a test. I must admit the pushing configuration works out well – extremely stable, perceptually faster, and definitely more interesting along the way, since we can climb back and forth between the raft and the boat.

When John arrives at Cabin Number 3 on the morning of our departure, his Hourston is loaded with camping gear, a big ice chest, and a few tools. I've already loaded the raft with a propane barbecue, two plastic chairs, and my camping equipment. Since his chainsaw is already on the front of his quad – now fully tarped onto the raft along with my quad –he asks to use my saw for a final raft modification.

"Need to cut a better notch on the back of the raft," he says. "We'll rope the Campion up tight so it won't shift around. See if you can find an old board we can use to support the bow of the boat."

While I look for a piece of lumber that's suitable to John, he finds a secure tie-up location for the boat's bow hook. He adds the two-by-eight I hand to him as a cross-board support. It's a skookum setup that will serve us well during our trip.

John adds rope supports running from each stern cleat of the boat to the brow log on the back of the raft. These will keep the raft tracking with the centerline of the boat. (Later, en route, we add a cargo strap to each of these ropes to allow us to adjust the tension of

John prepares the raft for bow of Campion

the lines.) All in all, the handling of the push-configuration far exceeds my expectations. Considering our previous disagreement on the topic, I reluctantly admit to John that he's right – again!

We load John's camping gear into the Campion, while I relocate mine under a tarp in the aluminum boat we'll tow behind us. I raise the outboard motor on the tin boat, and tie the 20-foot bowline of the boat behind the Campion. We'll have a spare boat to provide added cargo hauling capability and some extra fun during our visit to the Head. We pull out of Hole in the Wall, looking like pioneers moving to their new home in a floating wagon train.

"They must think we're hauling a nuclear bomb," I tell John, as one of the few boats on the lake today passes us slowly, looking closely at our tarped quads.

Our GPS speed settles down at 4.5 mph, which should get us to the Head faster than expected. We originally planned at least 7 hours for the trip, but now 5 seems possible. We should be there by late afternoon.

Departing Hole in the Wall

To prove his point that the push-method is superior to towing, John walks out onto the raft while I drive. Bro watches jealously from the bow of the Campion.

John and Bro on the trip north

The trip goes flawlessly, although the up-lake wind picks up when we begin the final stretch from Second Narrows to the Head. This is to be expected on a summer day, reminding us we'll need to leave early in the morning for the trip home. The whitecaps are a bit nasty, but they're pushing us from behind, so we take advantage of the extra speed and have no problem with control of the raft. Occasional bursts of water spray up from the bow of the raft and onto the tarped quads, but it's comfortable in the Campion.

We munch on our separately-packed lunches and talk over a multitude of issues we haven't had a chance to discuss in a long time. We don't solve any of the world's problems, but we try. We do piece together a few solutions to boat malfunctions involving our eleven mutual boats (some big, mostly small, all old, some engineless) that we operate (including kayaks and dinghies). Or at least we're convinced we've found a better way to do things than the manufacturers. Not once do we suggest reducing the number of boats, but we do discuss adding at least two prospective models to our mutual inventory someday soon, a 19-foot Harbercraft outboard and a small Lasar sailboat. And one of these days, maybe, a landing craft.

* * * * *

WHEN WE ARRIVE AT THE HEAD, there's no activity at the logging dock, so we pull right into the prime off-load position against the main dock. The Head has been shutdown for logging and the Plutonic power line construction project has been finished for almost a year. This spot was once a full-fledged logging camp, and I'm amazed that all of the buildings have been removed. There's little evidence anything or anyone resided and worked here, except for the big dock and plentiful dirt logging roads. A red pickup sits in the parking lot near the dock, maybe abandoned when the loggers moved out.

John gets to work right away building a ramp to off-load our quads. We could use the established barge ramp, but the empty dock will be even easier. He'll use the metal truck ramps we brought with us to bring the quads off the raft. With the addition of wooden ramps constructed from old boards found in the Head's parking lot, our quads are able to gently drop down over the rail of the dock.

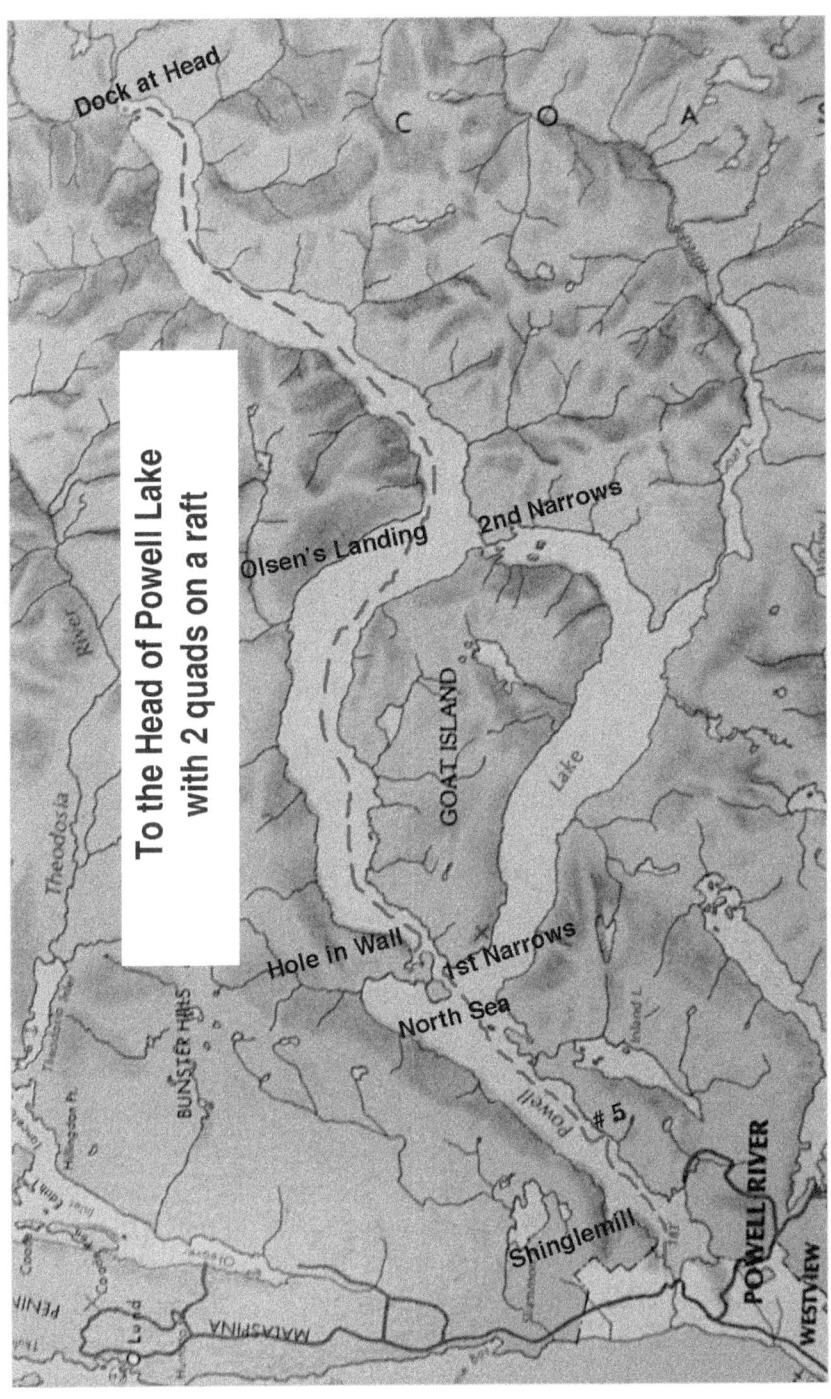

Unloading at the Head

I help move the ramps into position for each of the quads, while John starts up each bike in sequence, and drives them up and onto the dock.

We set up our tents on the dock, but there's no "ground" to pound in stakes. A strong wind could (and does) develop during our stay, so we decide to use nails as temporary anchors for the tents.

"Maybe we should test out our quads," I suggest as soon as our tents are secured.

I don't have to speak twice. John nods, and heads straight to his bike, which he has parked in front of mine. He lifts Bro aboard his aft box, and starts his quad. I'm similarly quick to get going, especially considering my normal snail's pace of getting started on a quad. But my bike starts only after extended cranking, and then it runs rough and dies. I restart the engine, but it still isn't running right.

"Maybe you should adjust my idle jet," I say. "Seems like it's running awfully rich."

"Add a little throttle," he suggests, talking back over his shoulder, while his engine idles smoothly.

"I tried that. It helps, but I'm going to wear out my thumb. Can't we adjust the idle?"

John turns off his engine, and walks back to my quad. He immediately reaches down below my left hand and turns off the choke, which was half on.

"Try that," he says, disgustedly.

The bike now starts and idles fine now, of course.

"Hey, that's no fair," I say. "You're the one who left my choke on when you took the bike off the raft. Not my fault."

"Yes, it is," he says, as he turns and walks back to his quad.

Case closed.

We drive up to the bridge, stop, and look down at the raging rapids emptying into Powell Lake. This is the true Head, as far as you can go on this lake by boat.

We explore a few side roads this first evening, not going very far. It'll be fun over the next few days to have our bikes right at our campsite. Want to exercise our quads? We're ready to go!

* * * * *

DINNER FOR ME CONSISTS OF A HAM SANDWICH and some tapioca pudding, plenty for my appetite tonight. Meanwhile, John cooks up three big hamburgers on the barbecue – two for him and one for Bro. He also prepares a full skillet of sliced potatoes, which he shares with me. They look delicious, but I only accept when I realize he has cooked way too many, even for his typically huge appetite.

It's almost dark now, but we still have time for a ride in the tin boat. John drives while I rig up my collapsible fishing pole. He maneuvers past the numerous snags that permeate the Head, almost to the bridge where we looked down on the rapids this afternoon. There seems no way to keep the boat in position in the strong whitewater, but John finds a spot where the back-current coupled with the normal downstream flow keeps us nearly steady. He shifts the outboard motor into neutral and we drift to and fro, never moving more than a few metres in any direction. I toss my small yellow spoon into the current and pull it through what looks like perfect trout water. I get several quick strikes, but they feel small, and none stay on my hook. Still, it's a thrill to be fishing here, right up next to the roaring inlet.

By dark, we're back at the dock, ready to watch some of the evening stars, and hopefully catch a glimpse of the Perseids meteor shower, now three days before peak. The Perseids can be spectacular, even slightly off maximum. This year, the sky will be moonless, and this is the perfect dark-sky location to see meteors. Today's trip to the Head has been nearly perfect in every respect. So why shouldn't we expect a spectacular celestial show?

Meteors pop into view several times a minute, just as advertised. Life doesn't get any better than this.

Camping on the dock

* * * * *

THE NEXT MORNING, we sleep until 8:30. I arise first, and start up my quad to move it off the entrance to the bridge to shore where it was parked beside John's bike overnight. Our parking scheme was partly to block the bridge from bears and partly to keep Bro from wandering off the dock during the night. We stored our trash bag in the back of the red pickup truck to divert bears from our sleeping area, and I pushed the barbecue with its food smell away from our tents, too.

We don't expect trouble from bears or cougars, but we know they're nearby. During our brief drive the previous evening, bear scat was everywhere, and fresh.

I awoke to Brody's growls a few times during the night, but they never grew to bear-siren proportions. If bears are in the vicinity, Bro will smell them, and go into his high-pitched shriek. It's a sound that's both annoying and comforting at the same time.

John is up now. He moves his quad away from the bridge, and lights the barbecue to fix his breakfast, a bowl of soup. Since he has an aversion to milk, this is the best he can do without a major cooking operation. Meanwhile, I eat cereal and milk. We don't want to delay getting going on our ride this morning, so a quick breakfast will help.

"There's a boat," says John, looking down the lake. "Must be coming here."

There's really no other place the boat could be headed. But I'm displeased at the invasion to our privacy. The logging operation is shut down, so who could this be?

The old hard-topped 20-foot fiberglass Lynnwood, *Daniels Lady*, probably named after nearby Daniels River, pulls into the dock area next to us. From the yellow boat, two men emerge, donning big backpacks and strapping on belts with multiple tools dangling from them. They look like loggers or road builders, and they head for the red pickup truck with barely a "Good morning."

"I'd better get our trash bag," says John. "We left it in the back of their pickup."

"See if you can find out who they are," I reply, wanting to know the details, but preferring that John ask the questions.

When John comes back with the trash bag, he explains they're surveyors who plan to lay out log falling boundaries on Cypress Main.

"They say logging will start up here again in a few months," he reports. "But they'll bring in a barge for the brief cutting operation. The camp here will probably never operate again."

It's a sad ending for a slice of logging history that's been a part of Powell Lake for a hundred years. Camps everywhere have shut down, victims of the efficiency of boat travel these days. Locally, the Head is where logging is remembered as a camp activity, and it's difficult to imagine it being over. When loggers go into an area, we complain. When they leave, we complain again.

The surveyors are at the truck for quite a while, and I don't hear it start. So I offer my opinion.

"Maybe they're having trouble getting it started," I suggest. "Why don't you offer to help? I'm sure you know more about trucks than they do."

"Maybe," says John.

There's no doubt John knows more about vehicles of all kinds than anybody I've met. And he's always generous with his assistance. Finally, after a few more minutes, he walks up to the red truck to see what's happening. He barely disappears over the bridge to shore before he reappears again, walking back towards our tents.

"Didn't want any help," he says. "Not very friendly about it either. They had the hood up, kinda' secretive, but said they know how to get it started. So I left."

That's strange. They may get the truck started, but it's already been quite awhile. Other than a dead battery, which isn't improbable, they'd need to be mechanically talented to get it fixed without extra parts.

Now one of the surveyors walks back past us to the yellow Lynnwood. He emerges with a small crescent wrench in his hand, and walks promptly back towards the truck. When he passes us, he stops briefly.

"How long you here for?" he asks, sounding friendly now.

"Three days," I reply. "It looks like you could stay for a month."

"No," he laughs. "We just carry a lot of equipment. What you're doing looks like fun."

"We've looked forward to this for a long time," says John. "Now we're finally here."

Then the man walks back across the bridge. I almost asked him what he plans to do with the wrench, but suddenly it dawns on me so I didn't need to inquire.

"Don't you think it's kind of strange how he went back to his boat for a tool as specific as a small crescent wrench?" I ask John.

"Sure is. Can't figure it out. It's as if they know exactly what's wrong."

"They do," I reply. "I bet their pickup has been disabled on purpose, so guys like you don't try to drive it around."

Just then, the pickup roars to life, sounding perfectly healthy. It's wise to disable your vehicle when it's going to sit unprotected in a remote area. Someone might play with it while you're gone. Thus, the wrench and the seeming disinterest in John's offer to help. Sometimes people are perfectly friendly, though they have their reasons not to seem that way at first glance.

While I pack what I'll need today onto my quad, I hear the truck rumble across the bridge above the rapids, and then down the road paralleling the opposite shoreline. A cloud of dust follows their path, with an occasional glimpse of the truck itself. The vehicle rattles as it hits potholes, continues farther down the main, and then starts up the steep road called Cypress Main. I watch them negotiate a switchback, still shrouded in dust.

When we're both packed and ready to go, I start my quad. This is a momentous occasion. Never did I seriously dream I'd ride my quad into the high country at the Head. The trip up the lake, in itself, has been a major adventure. Now we're headed up into the high country.

We ride uphill past the old gas depot, and then through the intersection leading to the bridge. We bear to the left, and begin our climb up Daniels Main. I ride to John's left, only a few metres behind him, the two of us taking up the whole road. This is a safe way to ride under today's conditions. I'm out of the dust swirl from John's quad and there's no one to meet head-on. The only other traffic on the entire road network is farther south – the surveyors on Cypress Main. I don't even bother to turn on my headlights as I normally do when riding on logging roads.

John honks his horn, and comes to a stop, while I pull up next to him. He has something to say.

"You know what? It took me eight years to finally get here."

What he really means is it has taken eight years to get his quad here. We've ridden here before, at least in the lower reaches, on our small 100cc motorcycles. But a quad is the vehicle that serves this region best. So this is a momentous day for John.

By the time we've driven another kilometre, Bro begins to whine – a loud piercing sound similar to his bear-siren. Either his nose has already detected some significant wildlife, or he's just being ornery this morning.

John pulls to a stop, helps Bro down from his aft-mounted box, and then lifts him (a very big dog) onto the seat of his quad. I've seen John do this once before when Bro was getting very tired from riding. John will now drive with Bro on his lap for a few kilometres, before returning him to his box. It's an awkward position for John, but Bro is entirely satisfied in this configuration. Spoiled brat. Or maybe he really did smell a bear.

Day # 2 - Bro on quad

After the split in the road where Powell Main takes off to the right (we stay to the left), we proceed to the Daniels Main 6-mile marker, where John spots a lake he's looking for.

"There it is," he says, as we come to a stop. "Right through those trees. I don't know if there's a way to hike in easily, but we'll look for one."

We drive along the main slowly now, inspecting the shoulder for breaks in the bushes. The growth is thick, and would be a struggle all the way down to the lake. Finally, John gives up on the prospect, and we throttle back up to normal speed.

An old landslide temporarily stops us, necessitating a short but rough stretch of almost-a-trail that dumps us back onto the main. I remember this landslide from several years ago when John and I road our small motorcycles here. The road is still passible, although only barely. If it weren't for the recent power line project that used the main, the road would have been entirely grown over already. So far, the main hasn't been officially deactivated, but that's probably only because there are so few recreational users in the area. Or maybe the logging company has plans for cutting here again in the near future. (By 2014, this main is fully reactivated and the site of a major logging operation.)

"They don't need roads to maintain the power lines," says John. "They'll just let the roads deteriorate, and bring in a helicopter if they need to do any repairs on the lines."

Farther up the main, we parallel the high wires that lead up and over to Toba Inlet where the electricity is generated in a run-of-the-river power project.

"Toba is right over that ridge," says John, pointing to where the Plutonic's lines go up to the saddle at the top.

Daniels Main power lines to Toba Inlet

Daniels Main

It's hard to imagine Toba Inlet can be so close. The only other way into Toba is by boat, and it's a long, circuitous trip from Powell River.

Precipitous peaks, glaciers, and dramatic waterfalls straddle the upper region of Daniels Main. It's a magical place, and we're the only people within many kilometres.

Daniels River

The river we're paralleling also provides a beautiful scene. We often look down on rapidly flowing water through breaks in the trees, and stop at several spots where we can access it.

At one of the gaps in the trees, John finds a trail we can follow all the way down to the river. At the bottom, the river spreads into a wide swath, split into two branches by a sandbar in the middle. The water is shallow, so we ride through it, out onto the bar.

Sandbar on Daniels River

Daniels River is highly photogenic, including a bridge scene I almost used on the front cover of my first book about off-road travel, *Up the Main*. In the end, I selected another picture for the cover. My original photo included motorcycles. This year's picture portrays my quad poised on the bridge.

In a few more kilometres, John pulls off the main, into a rough turnout.

"Do you remember this spot?" asks John.

How could I forget? During our motorcycle trip, I pulled over here to wait for John, who was intent on riding ahead to the end of the road (*Up the Main*, Chapter 18). I tried resting in the sun, but

Daniels Main Bridge

was attacked by mosquitoes so bad they bit me through my pants and successfully entered my helmet through its mouth opening. Mighty determined mosquitoes.

We continue past the infamous mosquito haven, feeling fortunate on this trip that these insects have had minimal impact, so far, even in the bush. The Plutonic-maintained portion of the road has now ended, and only the old logging road leads northward. It's narrower and green-canopied, tapering and lowering above us as we progress. Finally, the road ends where the old bridge has vanished. We can ride no farther.

So now we turn round and descend back down the main. I ride considerably behind John, wanting to travel slow and just absorb the fantastic scenery.

When we return to the intersection with Powell Main, we make the turn, not expecting to get very far. This road wasn't used during construction of the power lines, and logging has been absent on this

Daniels River

road for several years. In a short time, logging roads are reclaimed by nature, faster than one might imagine.

We stir up grouse all along the roads today. Sometimes Bro barks a warning that allows us to watch the birds spring up, often stumble-flying across the road in their awkward style. At other times, our bikes stir the grouse before Bro detects them, and they come so close to us that it frightens me a lot more than it frightens them.

John leads me off Powell Main, down a rough trail ending near the confluence of Powell River and Daniels River. Deep pools and tumbling water with a colorful granite bottom remind me of private garden pools. But few have seen these remote, swirling bodies of water. I use my collapsible pole to toss a few casts, immediately catching a few small trout. John says its okay to let Bro eat them. He accepts, gobbling the small fish in a few gulps, head and all.

Back on the main, bushes and tree branches encroach onto the road, making it narrower and narrower. Soon we must ride single-file, with alders closing in until we can't ride any farther. Then we turn around and battle our way out again.

On the way back to our campsite, John takes me on one more side-trip to his "secret spot." Rick and John discovered this location when they hiked from the old logging camp. So there's a hint – it's possible to hike to this secret spot from the dock. Another hint – Rick and John have extraordinary hiking endurance, so I can only tell you it's somewhere within the southern part of the province.

When John sights his prize location, we stop by the side of the road. Plunging white water is visible through the trees, still well upstream from where he seems determined to enter the bush.

"This is where Rick and I went in. It's a fairly easy climb, if you do it along the river, but it's pretty far to hike. Let's see if we can find a way in farther up this hill."

We get back on our quads, and drive very slowly a short distance up the road, while John cranes his neck to select the best spot to enter the dense undergrowth, which looks impenetrable to me. The place we park seems among the thickest of challenges. Nevertheless, it's time to swab on some bug juice, grab our packs, and push on through. As soon as we're a few metres off the road, the brush is well over our heads, and the groundcover is rough. Bro tries to lead the way, but he makes little progress.

We're hiking downhill now, approaching the river (which river is part of the secret), and big trees above us now protect the forest floor, making the sparser undergrowth less of an obstacle. We trudge through smaller bushes, though the ground is uneven and challenging. To sprain an ankle here could ruin my whole adventure, so I lag behind John and Bro, carefully watching every step I take. I try to keep an eye on John, not because I might lose him, but because there's good lessons in every step he takes. If I can keep my feet in his path, I'll make it through.

When we break out at the river, we're greeted by an easy drop down to wide granite slabs and pools of inviting cool water just above a waterfall. And we're seeking cool now, after sweating our way through the bushes.

It's a scenic spot for a refreshing swim, and John and I repeatedly slide into the water, and then back to lounge in the warm sun on the granite, and then into the water again. Bro slaps around in a shallow pool, where the glint of a darting trout keeps him busy. This isn't a place to stray too far from shore, since the current above the falls is significant. Our brief swims consist more of wading out to chest-deep water, and then briefly dipping our bodies into the glacial flow. In and out quickly, with only short bursts of dog paddling.

The rough hike was well worth it. I lie stretched out on my back on the warm granite, soaking wet and absorbing the sun's heat. My mind wanders to thoughts of how few people ever experience a swim at such a majestic location. Such is the nature of secret spots.

Secret Spot

* * * * *

WHEN WE DRIVE INTO THE WIDE GRAVEL LOT marking the old staging area for the logging camp, strong winds howl from the south, pushing whitecapped waves against the dock. The typical summer up-lake winds are substantial at the Head, reminding me we'll need to get an early start when it's time to head home. Today, at 4:30 pm, the winds are blasting our tents. If they weren't nailed down, they'd be gone.

The red truck is back in its parking spot, and *Daniels Lady* is gone. On the dock, the wind provides an appreciated cooling affect on a very hot day.

An hour later, as we prepare our dinner, the wind is substantially reduced, which raises another scenario contrary to an early-morning departure when it's time to go. We could wait until later in the evening when the winds finally subside. But that would be chancy, since a strong breeze could draw out until after-dark.

Evening #2

After dinner, we take a few minutes to kick back and enjoy the calmer conditions. John stretches out on his back, catching a catnap, using a dog as his pillow.

"This is the time of day when bears come out," says John. "I bet they're walking down the road right now."

A Man and His Dog

This is a hint, and I'm quick to grasp it.

"Why don't we go for a ride before dark?" I suggest.

John leaps up from his dog-pillow in an instant, startling Bro who springs up next to him.

"Let's go!" says John.

It takes us just a few minutes to motor out of the logging camp. We cross over the bridge and along the shore on the other side of the Head. We're crusin' for bear, with Bro standing guard as our warning siren. I call him our personal DEW Line – Distance Early Warning.

We cross Jim Brown Creek, then up towards a huge slash, riding slowly, scanning in all directions. At the entry to the slash, we stop and scrutinize the open area. Bears are often sighted in terrain like this, where they come out into the unsheltered area to forage for berries.

We drive slowly up a logging spur that climbs high into the slash. Deep trenches across the road slow our progress. It's a leisurely climb, with a brief stay at the top to look down on the Head.

Evening bear ride

Tonight, in a region where bears are plentiful, we ride for over an hour without seeing a single wild animal. It's a pleasant end-of-day sojourn, but our DEW Line doesn't issue a single alert.

* * * * *

Back at the dock, we sit in our plastic chairs, watching the sky as the first stars pop into view. A few Perseids streak briefly into view, now two days before peak. When full darkness arrives, we're treated to a real show.

"Wow!" we yell simultaneously, when a bright meteor blazes all the way from the north sky to an explosive end near the southwest horizon.

"There goes Lund," says John.

We stay up late, waiting for one more meteor to streak overhead. Lund, as far as I know, survived the show.

Chapter 3

Bear Siren
Head of Powell Lake

The next morning, we're on the road early, travelling the opposite shoreline from the dock, heading south towards Jim Brown Main. Brody's DEW Line is activated, blasting its high-pitch siren constantly for about two kilometres. Bear scat is fresh on the road, and there's little doubt he smells a bear. Suddenly, the siren goes silent just before we reach the beginning of the steep uphill climb.

After our previous evening ride, John went out again for a ride with Bro, while I remained at our campsite. When he returned, he reported seeing a bear looking down at him from the cliffs near the old gas tanks, which coincided with the spot where Bro's DEW Line was activated the day before during our first ride.

"That bear must live there," says John. "Probably he doesn't move around much, and Bro smells him whenever we go near."

Today, right after we start up Jim Brown Main, John looks back towards the dock, and sees the yellow surveyor's boat. He points it out to me, but I can barely see the dock from this distance, to say nothing of a boat.

"Those guys are back again," says John. "I wonder where they're going today."

"If it's Cypress Main again, maybe we'll see them there."

"Could be," replies John.

Cypress Main is on today's agenda. But for now, we cross Jim Brown Creek, and then head up Jim Brown Main to find the place where the new power lines go over the mountain saddle into the

Eldred River Valley, northeast of Goat Lake. John has climbed nearly to the top on the Eldred side, but couldn't get high enough to see down towards the head of Powell Lake.

If there's anything more plentiful than bear scat in this area, it's fireweed. The brilliant red blossom is plentiful this time of year, particularly in the higher altitudes.

We're able to follow the power lines to their final climb towards the saddle, but then the road ends, blocked by high mounds of boulders placed intentionally to prevent lookie-loo's like us.

"We could make a trail around these rocks," says John. "It would take us just a few minutes to get through. But why bother? You can see more piles farther up the road. There's one, and there's another."

He's pointing to specific spots in the main beyond this immediate pile of boulders, but I can't really see the obstacles he's pointing to.

"Maybe we could walk it all the way to the top," I say. "Then we'd be looking down on the Eldred."

"Not sure about that. It would be a tough climb, with the road ending not very far ahead. Then it's just the jumble of logs and rocks

Power line to Eldred River

below the wires. Besides, it could be just a level spot where the power poles seem to disappear up there. I bet it goes up for a lot of klicks after that."

His description reminds me of trying to top a high bank of clouds in an airplane. You climb ever higher, thinking there's just one more layer to surmount before you're in clear skies above. But after you clear one saddle in the clouds, there's another one ahead, even higher. Pilots call them sucker holes, and I can visualize the same situation here.

As we ride back down Jim Brown Main, I become complacent. I'm feeling comfortable, riding a bit faster than conditions permit, and suddenly come to a cross-trench that seems to jump out in front of me. Of course, if I'd watched the road closer, it would've been fairly easy to see. But in the morning shadows, ditches can blend in with the road, especially when trees cast shadows that sometimes falsely look like obstacles.

I see the trench at the last minute, early enough to hit the brakes, but late enough to carry too much speed into the dirt channel. I'm tossed upward from my seat, catching my thighs on the bottom of the handlebars, which slams me back down onto my seat again. I feel the bars dig into my legs. They will be bruised and sore tonight. It's an important reminder to slow down and keep my eyes focused on the road.

"Watch it!" says John, when I catch up with him.

He misses nothing – even when he's riding in front of me. John drives with both eyes fully concentrated on the road, but with his third eye on the rearview mirror, and his forth on the surrounding scenery. I can never get away with anything.

At the bottom of the road, we transition onto Cypress Main, which initially runs parallel to the lake, southbound. Bro's DEW Line siren begins to wail. We come around the next wide curve, and there's the bear.

This is an impressive creature, bigger than any bear I've seen before. It immediately stands up on its rear feet, making the creature seem even bigger – a typical action for a grizzly bear. But this is black bear territory, not where I'd expect to find a grizz. I've seen lots of black bears in this region, but never one of these. And he's jaw-dropping awesome.

We come to a complete stop, not having a choice. The bear stands upright on its hind feet right in the middle of the road, focused on us, and not intending to let us pass. This is the bear's road, and we're not about to argue about it. Well, maybe a little.

The bear sits back down on its haunches, no longer stretched as tall, now taking on a kangaroo-like look. But its big ears and previous standing pose convince me I'm looking at a grizzly bear. I don't see the telltale shoulder hump of a grizz, but there's otherwise no doubt in my mind.

Cypress Main bear standoff

"It's a grizz," I say to John over the continuing howl of Bro.

"Yup" is his curt replay.

Meanwhile, John is partly intent on the bear, and partly occupied with Bro, who is frantically trying to get off the bike. We're both afraid the dog will jump down from his box (not an easy chore for the heavyset pooch), and go tearing after the bear. It could be suicide.

Meanwhile, I'm thinking it would be good to turn around and go back the way we came. But I don't want to maneuver back and forth in this narrow road, and then expose my back to this animal. Nor is backing up a pleasant prospect, considering a quad's difficult control and low speed in reverse gear.

The bear is on all fours now, pacing slowly from one side of the road to the other, but never backwards in a retreat. In fact, the big bear is taking a few steps towards us.

Bear standoff

John shifts into neutral, revs his engine, and honks his horn. I don't have a horn, but I flash my headlights on and off. The bear keeps pacing back and forth, never letting its gaze leave a sight probably never seen before – two big humans on top of four-wheeled vehicles, with a black dog jumping up and down in the back seat, howling up a storm.

Besides the initial traits that make me sure this is a grizzly, this big animal is decidedly light brown. I've heard there are brown black bears, but I've never seen one. Certainly a brown one is rare, but not for a grizz.

John shifts back into gear, and guns his throttle, while controlling his approach to the bear with his brakes. The sudden movement seems to affect the bear. It finally takes a step backward and eases towards the side of the road. Then the grizz steps into the bushes and is gone.

Bear standoff continues

We wait a few minutes, and then continue down the road. I accelerate as we pass where the bear slipped into the bushes, getting past the spot as quickly as possible. Along here we see the tire tracks of the surveyor from the day before and maybe also earlier today. When we stop for a brief break, I ask John about the tracks.

"Those guys must have quite a battle with their truck, considering these cross-trenches," I say.

"Close to bottoming out, but it'll get worse ahead."

"Do you think they're up here again today?"

"Only two sets of tracks – one going up and one back down. They must have gone somewhere else today."

The tracks, although clear, are far from definitive to me regarding how many sets are present. So I ride the rest of the morning with my lights on, in case we meet an oncoming truck. I've gotten used to not seeing anyone on the roads around here, so someone coming the opposite direction could be an unexpected surprise.

The higher we climb on Cypress Main, the deeper the trenches. The tire tracks continue, but I imagine a jarring ride for the truck, with occasional bottoming-out. And the climb must have taken a long time, since the surveyors would have to slow to a crawl across these ditches.

Finally the tracks end, and to our right is a hanging collection of fluorescent red falling tape used to designate logging boundaries. We continue farther up the main, where the ascent is even steeper, climbing through swaths of thick forest sporting scenic waterfalls.

Cypress Main waterfalls

Then, even higher up, the main becomes wide open where it winds along a tall cliff to our right that looks down on a gorgeous valley. From the mountain slopes of nearly vertical granite on the opposite side, waterfalls plunge in ribbon-like S-turns. In the bright late-morning sun, the twisting falls look like tin foil, bright side up, leading to pools and meandering streams in the valley below. Steep stretches of pure rock on the higher peaks sport small glaciers feeding the waterfalls.

"Wouldn't it be great if we could get our quads up there," says John when we stop at a turnout overlooking the valley.

"That flat rock near the glaciers actually looks easy to navigate," I reply. "But how would we get up there?"

"Chopper."

"Oh, sure. That would be cheap."

"Hey, man, it'd be worth it."

Worth it? – yes. Feasible with quads? – not so much.

At a turnout where we pause for a few minutes, motors running, mosquitoes buzz around my helmet, only a minor attack in an area where a bug swarm would be expected. This summer began late, but then changed to an extensive stretch of near-perfect weather, and it

The Head from upper Cypress Main

seems to have affected the bugs. Good for people hiking and riding on quads and motorcycles, but maybe not so good for the environment.

Cypress Main ends in a small logging slash, the most majestic high view we'll experience during our visit to the Head. Looking down on the northern tip of Powell Lake makes the Head look like a small pond.

We descend back down Cypress Main leisurely, although I find myself accelerating a little through the spot where we encountered the bear. Once we're at the bottom, we join Falls Main, and start uphill again. In the first kilometre, we come face-to-face with the red truck parked in the middle of the road, pointed downhill, with nobody to be seen. When you know you're the only truck in entire system of logging roads, there's really no reason to pull off to the side when you park.

We easily navigate around the truck, and then continue our climb. John slows as we round a corner and approach a steep slope, where I catch up to him and stop to talk.

"Does this look familiar?" asks John, pointing to the turnout.

"How could I forget?" I answer, my mind clicking in with a not-so-pleasant memory of my previous incident here on my small motorcycle.

"Well, don't do it again," scolds John, knowing it would be nearly impossible on a quad.

This is the place where I wiped out on my 100cc motorbike, with minor facial lacerations. Now that's its history, it seems rather humourous, but certainly not at the time.

We pass the spot where we hiked into the snow survey cabin on our earlier trip to the Head. Today, we plan to climb higher, and then hike down to the cabin on a newer and shorter trail. This route takes us below mysterious-looking Slab Rock (as named by John – I call it the Great Wall of the Head), where giant granite swaths were ground smooth in the last ice age.

The hike down to the snow survey cabin is rough but quick. Bro insists on leading us on a thorn-infested route, which we follow so we don't lose him. High on the trees, yellow metal placards indicate the blazed trail, which parallels Bro's preferred path.

"They must have stood on top of really deep snow to pound in those yellow markers," says John.

The placards now stand about 10 metres above the ground.

We eat our lunch at the cabin, which is still in wonderful shape. It shows the durability of yellow cedar as construction material, even in the harshest of environments. This cabin is now a recreational stop for hikers, no longer used for the regular snow surveys from the paper mill. In the early 1900's, it was the only way to determine the stored winter water reserves for the lake, allowing forecasts for electrical power generated at the mill's dam. Back then, a day's boat ride to the Head was required, with the first night spent at another cabin at lake level. The second day would be a challenging winter hike up to this cabin, then another day back down to the lake and then south to the mill.

"They use helicopters now," says John. "Can do it all in a few hours rather than four days."

After we leave the cabin, we return to our bikes and ride up as far as we can go, where huge waterfalls plunge down from the big mountains even higher above us. More substantial glaciation is evident here, with Slab Rock remnants even more extensive.

A big fallen tree finally stops us, blocking the main. We could chainsaw our way through, but it'd take awhile. Besides, John says this road ends only a few hundred metres beyond this spot. Since he's never been here before, how does he know these things? He talks to others before he travels to new locations, and makes sure he figures it all out in advance. Of course, there are few places in this region he hasn't been, so he thoroughly researches the few places he's never visited before he goes.

On the way back down the main, we make two stops where John hikes off the road to explore a small pond on one side of the road and the river on the other side. I stay by my quad, soaking up some high altitude sun, taking some notes for this chapter, and photographing the Great Wall of the Head. John has told Bro to stay with me, which is obeyed with reluctance by the big dog. He paces beside my bike, waiting for his master. Again, there are almost no bugs here, so we luck out again.

Falls Main – Slab Rock

Continuing down Falls Main, we come to the red truck again. This time, three surveyors are packing their gear into the truck bed, ready to climb aboard and begin their descent. We stop and discuss their previous days rugged trip through the deep trenches of Cypress Main and our encounter with the bear.

"This ol' truck takes us anywhere we need to go," says the youngest of the three surveyors. "It just keeps plugging along, even though we give it lots of abuse. So where exactly did you see the bear?"

"Right after the intersection at the bottom of the hill, where Cypress Main parallels the shoreline," says John. "No more than a half kilometre past the junction."

"It sounds like a grizzly to me," says the surveyor. "Especially the part about standing up and defending its territory. Did you see a hump?"

"Not really, but it was light brown, and the ears were big like a grizzly," I reply.

"But if there wasn't a hump, it wasn't a grizz," says the young fellow. "Could have been a brown black bear. They're rare, and tend to be a bit ornery like this one."

"We need to go back up Cypress Main before we're finished today," notes another surveyor. "Not looking forward to meeting that guy."

We talk a little longer. John asks about a trapper's cabin on Daniels Main he's heard about. One of the men knows where it is, and describes it to us in terms of a place where the power lines cross the main. Supposedly, the cabin is right off the road; close enough to be visible through the trees.

The youngest surveyor, who seems to do most of the talking, kids us about our barbecue at the dock, asking if we'll have breakfast ready for them when they arrive tomorrow.

"We would if we weren't leaving at the crack of dawn," says John. "Gotta' get out before the winds come up the lake."

"Excuses, excuses," chides the young surveyor.

We leave before the men get into their vehicle, which will put us in front of them on the ride downhill, protecting us from their truck's dust. But John wants to explore one of the side spurs, and the surveyors go rumbling by while we're off the main road.

When we pull back onto Falls Main, John stops for me to catch up.

"I know where we're going," I say matter-of-factly.

"Back to the dock?" asks John, as if he doesn't know what I'm talking about.

"No, up Daniels Main to find that trapper's cabin."

"Okay, if you insist."

John is off immediately in a cloud of dust. I just knew he was determined to find the cabin, and now he's on a beeline for his target.

But we don't find the cabin at the power lines, assuming this is the right crossing point. We stop and walk into the woods, finding a lush park-like setting with big trees and high canopies that keep the ground cover minimal. But there's no evidence of an old cabin, and our search along the side of the power poles is also unsuccessful. We drive along the road in one direction, then the other, for at least a kilometre on both sides of the lines, looking between the trees as far as we can see. It isn't often that John misses his mark, but maybe the surveyor provided bad directions.

"Didn't he say on the north side of the power lines?" asks John.

"Actually, I wasn't paying close attention, because I knew you were."

"Ernie says he knows where the cabin is, so I'll ask him when we get home, and I'll find it next time."

Of that I have no doubt. John doesn't take failure lightly. And it's another example of how John researches trips like this in advance, talking to people like Ernie to hone in on his targets.

By the time we get back to the dock, the red truck is already parked, and the yellow boat is gone. The late afternoon wind is again strong, reminding us we'll need to get going early in the morning. So we decide to load up as much as possible tonight, easing our schedule in the morning.

John drives our quads back onto the raft, and after dinner we load the barbecue. But we have enough time before dark to get one more ride in the tin boat. John has seen several blue barrels along the shore just north of the dock. This is an area infested with snags, so we motor slowly towards the barrels. Both of them are cracked and unusable, but it takes nearly an hour to get close enough to both of them to determine their status. Then John seeks a submerged chimney of an old house used long ago as a tourist lodge before the dam at the mill raised the lake level. How he knows about this chimney, I'm not sure, but he somehow navigates our boat right over the site. Sure enough, the mortar walls of a big chimney are clearly visible below us. It's an amazing postscript to a wonderful three days of exploration.

*****

The next morning, we motor out of the Head in calm conditions, pushing the raft and pulling the tin boat. The trip goes comfortably, sneaking out of the upper arm of the lake before even a light breeze arises. Just past Second Narrows, we see *Daniels Lady* headed up the lake, closing fast. I'm sure they recognize us, since there isn't another raft with quads on it within many miles.

The yellow boat slows as it approaches, then maneuvers in close, reversing direction so it rides parallel with us at 5 knots. The young surveyor that did most of the talking steps out on the aft deck. I'm in the bow of the Campion, while John drives, putting me in the best position to carry on a conversation with a boat riding in formation.

"Hey, I bet you stopped here for breakfast," I say. "I'll step out onto the raft and get the barbecue going."

"No breakfast this morning," laughs the fellow. "We just had to stop to ask if you're Wayne Lutz."

"As a matter of fact I am," I reply, knowing what has happened.

I'm not famous in the Powell River area, but there's a bit of a cult following for my series of books. It's too bad that most of my local readers borrow the books from someone else. I don't sell many books here, but lots of readers in this region share them, passing them from uncle to nephew and every which way.

"After I got home yesterday, I thought about you guys," says the young fellow. "Then I remembered the dog in the back of the quad."

"Yes, that's us," I yell back over to the yellow boat. "Of course, Bro is hard to forget. John, too."

I motion towards John in the Campion's driver's seat, who now smiles back, accepting his normal fame as an infamous local character.

"You know," says the young fellow, "I think you ought to write a book about your trip to the Head."

"You know, as a matter of fact, I might."

Chapter 4

Following Logging Trucks
Theodosia Valley

AT 6:55 AM, my alarm clock rings me awake. I turn on the bedside radio, already tuned to the local FM station. In a few minutes, I'm groggily listening to the 7 o'clock news and local weather – mixed sun and clouds and a forecast high of plus 5. Not bad for mid-December.

By 7:45 I'm motoring out of the Hole under enough light to see the floating debris caused by the slowly rising water in the lake, common after recent rains. On mornings like this, I need to take it slow until I'm clear of First Narrows, since a rising lake pulls driftwood lodged on the shore into the main flow. At Hole in the Wall, the drift in and out under typically calm conditions in the early morning creates a considerable debris field. Boat hulls handle small floating wood with few problems, but propellers and legs not so well.

It's the standard routine for riding my quad, and it takes awhile to accomplish. First I must motor down the lake to the Shinglemill, and then load whatever I'm taking with me into my truck for the ride to the airport. Then it's through the locked gate, where I stop again to secure the entry behind me, before finally arriving at my quad trailer in the open-ended hangar that protects our bikes quite adequately from winter storms blowing through this area. And that's just to get started. Of late, trips like this have caused me to think about a new scenario – bringing my quad to Hole in Wall, where I can begin an off-road ride from my cabin. But today it's only a vague notion in the back of my mind.

I hook up to the trailer, which contains two quads, and pull forward. I'll off-load Margy's quad and lock it away in the hangar while I'm riding today. This will please John. Bringing both quads for a solo trip upsets his sense of equipment security.

I hop aboard the trailer, planning to start both quads and let them warm up, while I lower the off-load ramps to remove Margy's quad and prepare my gear for today's ride. Neither bike starts. I say to myself aloud: "Fuel? Ignition? Too cold?"

What should I do now? Rather than phone John, which is how I'd normally proceed, I decide to haul the trailer to his house and ask him to help me get the quads started. We're supposed to be going riding together, so I'm sure he'll be glad to help. When in doubt, take the equipment to the mechanic. Two quads with the same problem, simultaneously, seems a bit improbable. Yet here it is.

I'm on my way now, although hauling two dead quads. I stop to unlock the gate, and then halt again to bolt it behind me. Then I motor down the hill, pulling up behind John's house in the alley where I'll be less of an obstacle to traffic.

John hears me arrive, and bounds out the door. I'm quickly out of the truck and greeting him with the bad news: "I tried to off-load Margy's quad and leave it at the hangar, but I couldn't," I say when he's within shouting distance.

"What now?" he asks.

"Couldn't get it started," I say, while simultaneously climbing aboard Margy's silver bike for another try. "Couldn't start mine either."

"Neither one? Must be the cold. Did you use the choke?"

"Sure, but you're right," I reply. "Must be the cold."

Fuel, ignition, cold; I repeat to myself as I'm about to turn the key. Fuel? Wait a minute!

I look towards John, who isn't taking an immediate interest in my problem. Rather than walking over to my trailer, he's now sauntering towards the shed behind his house to retrieve his quad for loading in his truck. His back is turned to me, as he shouts over his shoulder: "Try 'em again. Maybe they've warmed up by now."

So I take advantage of his temporary disinterest, which certainly won't last long if the quads still fail to start. I reach down to the fuel valve. Of course, fuel! I twist the valve to the "On" position, flip the choke open, and crank the starter. Surely John hasn't caught me. *Vroom! Vroom!*

Before he reaches the shed, John turns to face me: "Got her!" he yells, pumping his fist in the air.

I seldom win this game, but today I've slipped one by him. So far.

"Must have warmed up in the sun during the drive down the hill," I say.

"Must be," says John. "Try the other one."

I hop onto my red quad, careful not to reach down for the fuel valve until I see John disappear into the shed. The quad fires right up, just like Margy's did. All it takes is a little fuel.

"Right on!" I hear John yell from inside the shed.

Yes, right on, I think to myself.

* * * * *

THE TRAIL INTO THEODOSIA is slightly improved since the last time I was here, although it's not exactly smooth access. From Southview Road, where we off-load our quads, it's an easy and beautiful ride, dropping down towards Okeover and Lancelot Inlets, and then up the park-like trail leading to Theodosia Valley. From there, it's a short stretch to the spot where the entrance to Theo often falls apart. It's never been easy here, where the trail drops down to the logging dock at Theodosia Inlet. The last part of this short trail (just above the dock) has always been challenging, but in recent years the top section of the trail has become the biggest problem. Every year it's a little different, part of the constant battle between quad riders and loggers regarding how this portion of trail should be arranged. Sometimes, it seems like the loggers are simply trying to get rid of us. Lately, it's been so rough in this section that I'm not sure Margy could get through. Yet it would be our primary route for bringing our quads to Hole in the Wall, as we plan to do soon. I expect, when and if the time comes, I'll need to drive her bike through this section while she hikes in on foot.

For my level of riding experience, it's a challenging entry to a demanding trail that tests my limits. I make it through today without a problem, following John and concentrating on where he places his wheels in the rutted curves. After we've made it through the most demanding section, John pulls well out in front of me, since he knows I can make it the rest of the way, and I'm even familiar with the route for a ways past the logging dock.

At the bottom of trail that dumps out at the dock, trucks are parked everywhere, with the sound of big rigs operating nearby. Trucks full of logs are waiting to dump their loads into the chuck. There are pickups, cranes, and more activity than I've seen here in years. The price of lumber is rising, and China is on a log-buying spree.

John is nowhere in sight, so I'm sure he's taken off down the road, knowing I'll follow. Thus, I'm riding solo when I almost immediately see a pickup coming in the opposite direction, with an arm out of the driver's window, waving me over.

"Lots of logging going on up the main," says the young supervisor.

He goes into a quick dissertation about where trucks can be expected and what logging locations are active today. I catch the name of few places I've heard of, but most of the descriptions are obviously local slang designations John would be familiar with. To me, it might as well be Portuguese.

"My friend, John, will need to talk to you," I say. "I really don't know this area, but I'm following him. I'm supposed to meet him at the first junction, so I'll send him back to talk to you."

"Okay. Be safe," says the fellow, almost immediately stomping down on his accelerator and leaving me in a literal cloud of dust.

I find John at the turnout to the point overlooking the inlet. He's sitting on his quad, looking inpatient.

"Did you see that white pickup just as you started out from the dock?" I ask.

"What about him?" he asks. "I saw the truck, and waved to him as I hustled over here."

"Well, he stopped to tell me about where they're logging today. I caught some of it, but I didn't recognize some of the spots he referred to. I heard a reference to Theo Main, but that's about it."

"No problem, we'll follow a truck," he replies.

"Don't you think it would be a good idea to go back and talk to him?" I ask. "It sounds like a lot of logging activity today."

"We'll just follow the next logging truck headed up the main," he reiterates.

I'm still a bit nervous, but John sits on his quad, still not attempting to start his engine. It seems to me, I'd best leave it alone.

Sure enough, in just a few minutes a big logging truck, now empty, approaches from the dock area, and John gives him a friendly wave that must somehow signal the driver to pull over. To me it looks merely like a "Hello," but the truck slows, pumps its air brakes with a single blast, and comes to a stop opposite us. John hops off his quad and jumps up onto the running board on the passenger side, while the truck driver reaches over to roll down the window.

I can't hear what they talk about, the noise of the diesel engine drowning out their conversation. But in a few minutes, John steps off the running board and heads back towards me, while the truck remains stopped.

"We'll follow him all the way to the cutoff. Just stay behind me, and pull off when I pull off. He's in radio contact with the trucks coming down the main, so he'll keep us clear of them."

"What happens when we get to the cutoff," I say, as if I know where that is.

"We're on our own from there. But there's no logging going on from there to the portion of Heather Main we'll be on. Besides, the snow will be too deep for us to go much farther."

Oh, now I get it. We follow this truck to a spot where we head off uphill until our quads get stuck in the snow. Then, I suppose, we turn around and find another truck to follow back to the logging dock. This looks like an all-day event. And you know what? – As usual, it'll undoubtedly be an adventure I'll love. It's always that way with John.

John gets back on his quad, and quickly starts it. He waves to the truck driver, and the big vehicle starts forward again. The truck is carrying it's own rear wheels on a rack behind the cab, going to a place where it'll pick up some more logs. Followed, for now, by two quads.

It works amazingly well. It's easy to keep up with the truck, and on this winter day there's little dust behind him. I can't imagine what this would be like on a dry day of summer, with the enormous clouds of dirt thrown up on these roads by a truck like this. But today it works efficiently.

After progressing about a klick, the truck's brake lights flash twice, the driver slows, and we all pull over to the right side of the road.

There's only enough space for the big truck to get far enough clear of the road to allow room for another vehicle coming down the main. But it's obviously wider than most sections of the road – a place where trucks in radio communication make arrangements to pass each other. I pull up behind John, who is now within arm's reach of the rear of the truck.

"See, it works fine," he yells over the noise of our engines and the diesel in front of us. Then he turns off his engine, and almost immediately the truck in front of us does the same. I too turn off my motor, and stillness surrounds us on the side of a road in the middle of nowhere.

We sit for several minutes, waiting for the down-the-main truck to appear, and finally it does. It's a big rig full of logs, barreling down the dirt road. At his high speed, probably at least 50 klicks on this congested section of the road, dust is flying furiously, even in today's winter-moist conditions. I imagine to myself that the driver in front of us has added a few extra comments during his radio conversation: "I've got two quads parked behind me. Give 'em a thrill."

And a thrill it is, as the big loaded truck rushes past, the driver waving to us. We wave back, restart our quads, and wait for the truck in front of us to move on out again. I feel like a running back on a football team, trained to score a touchdown: "Just follow your offensive blockers to the goal line. They'll get you there."

Two more times, before we reach the cutoff, our big "blocker" pulls off the side of the road, where we wait for whoever is coming down the main. First it's another loaded logging truck, and then a pickup carrying loggers down to the dock. In typical British Columbia fashion, the crummy transport blazes by at a speed that makes the vehicle seem intent on flying off the road.

When we leave our offensive blocker at the cutoff, we wave, and the driver honks his horn: "Thanks!" I yell.

He honks again, seemingly saying: "Any time, guys!"

For the rest of the trip up the main, I think about how pleasantly complex today has been, from the moment I heard the alarm ring. As I ride up Heather Main, I reflect on how nice it would be to avoid all of the complications of travelling so far from my cabin just to begin a ride on my quad. But I also try to imagine what it would be like if it was difficult to include John on my rides because they began at my cabin. How much I learn from him.

Should I follow through on my plans to bring our quads to Hole in the Wall? On this day, I'm not so sure. But I do know the day turns out as expected. John and I ride and ride until we can go no farther, for the snow on Heather Main becomes so deep we can no longer plow up the mountain.

So we get off our bikes and manhandle them around, facing back downhill. We head back down the main, and wait for another logging truck to lead us home.

Chapter 5

The Edge of the Wilderness
Haslam and Giovanno Lake

THE GOAL OF THIS BOOK is to capture quad adventures more remote and challenging than those in our local backyard. Yet, our own neighborhood is certainly not lacking in inspiration when it comes to off-road exploration. Nor are adventures difficult to find.

Take the Edgehill trail system, for instance. For years, I heard of quad riders beginning their rides in the parking area at the end of Abbotsford Street, adjacent to Edgehill School. My assumption was that this was where novices began their rides. Then I tried it myself.

The amazing thing about the Edgehill trail system is how easy it is to begin a ride from the edge of town, and immediately be immersed in the wilderness. From paved roads and a lively little city, suddenly you find yourself plummeting into tall trees. You're out of town in an instant.

My first ride from this parking area was with Margy in the early spring, climbing the Edgehill trails towards Duck Lake Forest Service Road. Just before joining the road, we turned right on the Washout Trail, heading down towards the Blue Trail. Pockets of white icy foam guarded both sides of the trail, seeming out of place in the relatively warm air. Was this really ice or some kind of fungus?

When Margy and I parked our quads and trekked towards one of the white patches, it became evident this was ice of a most unusual type – frozen vapor called hoar frost. This sublimated ice goes directly from gas to solid, and forms in limited locales near Powell River. Hoar frost is restricted to areas where the near-freezing air vapor contacts dead or damaged alder logs and branches. In our area, only alders harbour this unique frost that extrudes in fine, thin treads.

On another solo voyage into the Edgehill system on a winter day, I followed an extensive set of bear tracks that led me down one of the primary trails. Here, right on the edge of town, was the obvious habitat of a very large bear.

Bear tracks near Edghill School

Edgehill is a great place to immediately leave the city behind, and find yourself absorbed by the bush. It reminds me that the backcountry dominates the earth, and our pockets of population are carved out of a greater and omnipresent wilderness.

* * * * *

Margy hadn't ridden her quad in 11 months, and my riding hasn't been regular lately either. Sometimes life's challenges divert us from where we should be. Fortunately, we can return to the places we've temporarily left behind, as long as we take the time to remind ourselves that we can.

A sunny day in late July offers the perfect opportunity to break our mold of inactivity. The high temperature is forecast to be in the low twenties. Meanwhile, most of Canada and the States are mired in a persistent heat wave that makes national headlines. Locally, this is beginning to look like a year without a well-defined summer, all of which provides perfect quad riding conditions. Even the dust should be minimal, considering the regular rains that have moved through our area since summer began.

We unstrap our quads from the trailer, our truck the only one in Edgehill's wide parking area. The unusual summer conditions have scared a lot of people away, or maybe they're using today's unexpected sunny conditions to catch up on other pursuits delayed by the rash of unsettled weather. With only a few trailer restraint straps remaining to unhook, our friends, Dave and Marg, pull into the lot – a maroon truck pulling a maroon quad. Dave is the only guy I know who carries his passion for maroon further than me. Usually he tows his quad behind his other truck, a white vehicle that does most of the dirty tasks.

"There's nothing like a maroon quad," I say in greeting. "Wish I had one."

"How do you like our new truck?" says Dave.

"New truck?" I reply. "You mean you now have two maroon trucks?"

"Traded in the white one," he says.

He's definitely has me beat on the maroon obsession.

Their quad is one of the new Grizzlies with power steering, a special edition model, uniquely maroon. Today, Margy and I will ride our small Kodiaks, while Dave and Marg double on their Grizz. When I ride with Dave, I can expect to learn a lot about the region. He's my mentor when it comes to regional history and knowledge of the area's trail systems. As Powell River's current ATV Club president (extending now longer than any previous president), he's involved in almost every local project involving backcountry recreation.

Marg is similarly an expert on nature, one of the most knowledgeable backcountry women I've ever met, and always comfortable in wilderness settings. She's an accomplished hunter, with a freezer full of big game provisions to prove it, which is difficult to contemplate when you notice her small structure.

"Marg" is also my nickname for Margy – you'd think it would lead to confusion when the four of us are together, but it never does: "Hey, Marg, can you give Margy a hand with her quad?"

Marg is an experienced quad driver, though she'll ride "double" behind Dave most of today. Occasionally today, she'll takes control of the bike to drive it solo down rough stretches of trail, while Dave helps Margy maneuver through steep sections that test her personal limits.

To top it off, Marg and Dave are two of my all-time favourite people. Margy and I feel fortunate to ride with them today.

Margy (the other Marg!) is now aboard her quad on the back of our trailer, ready to start the engine and back her bike down the aluminum ramps. Like me, when she hasn't ridden for a while, she feels a bit uncomfortable. But she sets the choke, and gets her quad started without difficulty.

"Looks like she still remembers how to start it," I say to Dave.

Suddenly, Margy's quad quits.

"And how to stall it, too," I laugh.

When Margy tries to restart the engine, the starter cranks over fine but the motor fails to fire.

"Oh, try this," I say, walking back from my quad to hers.

I point at the fuel lever, and Margy moves it to the "On" position. (We never make the same mistake three times.)

"My fault," I admit. "I forgot to turn on the gas for either of our bikes."

We're each in charge of certain things. This was my error, but we survive, as usual.

Margy backs down the ramps, while I start my quad, and then back off the trailer, too. Meanwhile, Dave has driven his quad down his ramps. We all don our helmets and gloves, and we're ready to ride.

"Shall I lead?" I ask Dave.

Of course, this is a ridiculous question. Dave knows so much more about these trails than I do, and we all know he should lead.

"Sure," replies Dave, always easy-going, and ready for anything.

"Of course, there's no way to tell where we'll end up," I add.

I'm famous for getting lost, and Dave has seen some of the results first-hand.

"On second thought…" says Dave, pulling forward, ready to lead us into the forest. "…Here we go."

* * * * *

AS SOON AS WE LEAVE THE PARKING AREA, the forest absorbs us. Tall trees and a trail with muddy pools enhance the feeling that the city has been left behind – immediately. Dave and Marg ride in the lead position, followed by Margy, and then me. The arrangement is comfortable for all of us.

Once out on Duck Lake Forest Service Road, we pick up our pace, and there's a little dust. But compared to normal summer conditions, this is minor. On main roads today, a dust length spacing of twenty metres is adequate, which means on most stretches I never lose sight of either quad in front of me. On the narrower trails, there's no need to worry about dust at all. In fact, nearly everywhere today, the dirt has that dark look of moist soil.

At Duck Lake Bridge, we travel east, then north towards Haslam Lake. At several spot, Dave pulls to the side of the road and stops, motioning for us to come up beside him. Margy pulls a little forward of the maroon quad, while I tuck in close behind her, where we both can hear what Dave has to say.

"They're logging up the road," says Dave at one of our typical three-bike stops today, explaining that cedars are being logged near the Alaskan Pine cutoff. As ATV Club president, he considers it one of his personal responsibilities to keep up with what's going on throughout the regional system of mains and trails.

At other stops, he explains about the natural habitat and characteristics of wildlife that can be observed by keen eyes. Did I mention that Dave is also an expert regarding everything having to do with the forest environment, having worked in one of his (many) previous segments of life as a timber cruiser? A "cruiser" evaluates the growth environment of trees, timber quality, and falling boundaries relative to future harvesting.

As we ride along East Haslam Main towards the head of the lake, Margy comes to a screeching halt. Since I'm not paying adequate attention, I come to an even more screeching halt behind her, stopping within a few feet of her quad, while the maroon quad temporarily disappears around the curve in front of us.

"Bear!" she says, pointing over her shoulder towards the logging slash we've just passed.

I back up about 10 metres, and see the bear climbing the hill at the edge of the slash. Margy backs up, too, and we both watch a full-size adult bear climb up the hill until it enters dense bush and disappears. He (or she) doesn't seem to be in a hurry.

This is the first bear I've seen in nearly a year. Sometimes you can go on quad rides and see bears on back-to-back trips. At other times, you can go for a long time without seeing any. In fact, wildlife, in general, is like that. There are times when you don't see any ground animals, although you ride all day. Today will be one of those days when critters pop up here and there repeatedly along the trail.

Twice during the day, Dave and Marg come upon a family of grouse. During the second encounter, the mother awkwardly flaps her wings, and gets ahead of our quads, leaving her four babies bobbing along the side of the road. When she recognizes our bikes separate her from her brood, she becomes obviously disturbed. Dave drives slowly here, edging his way past the mother. We follow, barely moving, so as not to disturb her any more than necessary. When we finally pass the adult bird, she hurries back to her babies. All is well again.

Dave points out a series of elk prints in the dirt road, indications of a herd of Roosevelt Elk moving north. He's been involved in numerous government projects involving elk relocations in our area. He's assisted in trapping and moving the big animals to areas where they now thrive. In recent years, the relocation of Roosevelt Elk, after making considerable progress over the years, has totally halted due to

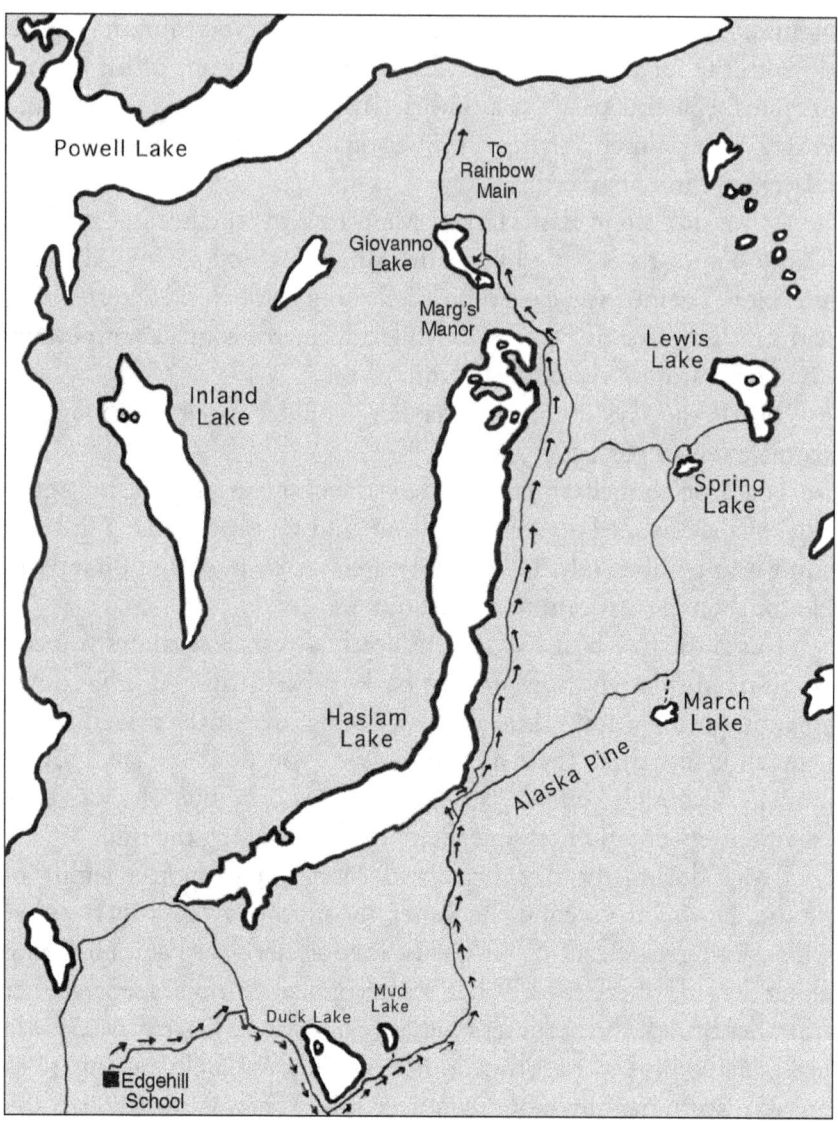

The Edge of the Wilderness

financial cuts in the program. When economies improve, maybe this important program will resume.

Our destination today is Marg's Manor on Giovanno Lake, initially built by Dave and Marg several years ago, and now improved by our local ATV Club and open to the public. The project included blazing the trail to the shoreline, construction of wooden benches, beach trails, tent platforms, and a dock. The hard work shows.

We ride past the head of Haslam Lake, then uphill onto Giovanno Main, to the turnoff for Marg's Manor. When we finally pull off the main, we start downhill across some big granite slabs and steep grades winding through dense growth. It's one of those trails that's both challenging and scenic, part of the typical wilderness experience on a quad.

Margy on trail

Margy is able to handle the first portion of the trail, but then gets bogged down at a curve that drops precipitously downhill. Dave has already stopped, and is walking back to assist, while Marg takes their maroon quad the rest of the way to the beach.

"It's a bit tight here," he says to Margy. "But within your capabilities. You'll need to follow the left side to get around a big root at the bottom of this part of the trail, down there."

Dave points to the area where the big root seems to block access to the lower section of the trail. From behind them, I can visualize the inside of Margy's helmet, where I'm sure her face registers concern. She wants to try it, but she feels it's beyond the limit of her abilities on a quad.

"I can ride your bike through this part, if you want," says Dave.

Margy immediately nods "Yes," and gets off her quad. She walks behind Dave as he maneuvers down this short stretch. I follow them down the hill, until Dave stops and relinquishes the controls to Margy again. Now he waves me past him, and then walks behind us down the last section of the trail.

In another 50 metres, we're at the end of the route, where a small parking area provides access to the beach. I pull up behind Marg on her maroon Girzzly, stopping next to Margy on her Kodiak. Three quads – maroon, silver, and red – at a scenic spot.

We sit on the skookum bench overlooking the lake, eating our lunch and enjoying our special friendship, while watching an ambitious snake slithering along the edges of the dock, seeking its prey. Meanwhile, a loon swims by in front of us, not seeming to notice the presence of humans. Dave cups his hands, and makes a loon call. The black and white bird cranes its long neck towards shore, dismisses the false intrusion with a quick stare at us, and then continues swimming along the shore.

As is typical of today, we get a close look at wildlife at the lakeshore site. On one of the hiking paths near the shore, we find a martin's den within a grove of fir and cedar "vets." These veteran trees (first growth) are rare in the forest these days, but here in Marg's Manor they stand tall and proud.

Red huckleberries, tart and not fully ripe yet, give the bushes added colour. Indian Pipe (an orchid) is just beginning to push up in a rich looking area of soil under the big trees. This pink flower is a unique plant – it grows entirely without chlorophyll, and is thus easily damaged by errant footsteps, which makes Marg's Manor the perfect place for it to remain protected from human neglect. There's something about this place that's exceedingly peaceful – tranquility in the vast wilderness, brought to life by caring people.

Dave & Marg at Marg's Manor

◊ ◊ ◊ ◊ ◊ ◊ ◊

Chapter 6

The Wednesday Crew
Theodosia Valley; Elk Lake

EVEN IN THE WINTER, I find it difficult to pull myself away from my floating cabin to ride. In the off-season it isn't so much wanting to be on the cabin's deck or boating on the water that interferes, it's the short days. If I go to town in the morning to ride my quad, it'll be difficult to return up the lake before dark. Of course, that's more of an excuse than a reason, since I can stay over in town, and riding is always wonderful once I get going. But getting going in the winter is a bit of a chore.

On a fairly warm February morning, I leave the cabin at 9:30, intending to ride by myself from the easily accessible Edgehill School off-load location. My plan is to spend a few hours exploring the trail to Granite Lake or the set of trails off Duck Lake Road. I doubt John will be interested in joining me, since it'll be a short trip, what I call one of my admittedly "wimpy rides." So I'll be able to doddle in my preparations, including breakfast in town and hooking up the trailer at the airport. But just to be sure John has the chance to join me (and for me to obtain some last-minute logging activity information), I come off plane in the Bayliner, and shift into neutral to use my cell phone.

"Hello," says the almost-John voice on the other end.

"This is Rick, isn't it?" I proudly announce, remembering how many times I've misidentified their voices previously.

"Yup. Hi, Wayne. How's it going?"

"Good. Just on my way down the lake, and wanted to check in to see if anyone there wants to go on a wimpy ride."

"Not me," replies Rick. "John's gone already, working for some lady."

This is enough to explain why Rick has answered John's phone. And it's not unexpected that John is out earning some money. Ladies are always contracting him for construction jobs, and I don't blame them. I'm sort of a lady myself, and I can't think of anyone I'd trust more to fix something for me than John.

"I was thinking of going up to Granite Lake, or maybe Coyote Lake, but I'm wondering about the logging activity."

"Nothing to worry about. Just keep your eye out for trucks after you leave Duck Lake. Most of the work now is farther down Granite Main, past the Granite Lake turnoff."

"What about Coyote Lake?" I ask. "Do you think I can make it that high today, or is there too much snow?"

"Doubt you can get all the way to Coyote. But you can probably make it to Granite. The snow is pretty high right now."

And it's been high most of the winter. No two winters are alike around here, and this one has been plenty mild, with less precipitation than normal and a lot less cold than the winter standard.

"Hey, can you go with me?" I suggest. "You can lead me on a good ride. I'd like that."

Although it's a weekday, Rick is still home during mid-morning, so maybe he's not working in his taxi today. He's one of the most renowned quad riders of the region, and there isn't anywhere he doesn't know like the back of his hand. I haven't ridden with Rick in a long time, so it would be quite an opportunity.

"No, I'm going to Theodosia," he replies. "The Wednesday Crew is fixing up the trail, and I want to help."

The Theo trail has been a real problem in recent months. Since last summer, it's been nearly unusable, at least by riders like me, due to logging road rerouting and sections with giant cross-trenches. On my last trip into Theodosia a few months ago, I made it through, but I determined it was beyond the level Margy would find acceptable. Since this trail is the only viable land route to Hole in the Wall on Powell

Lake, it's loss takes away quad access to our cabin. The only other route is the Last Chance Trail, much rougher by several magnitudes.

"I should help, too," I say. "That route is important to me, and I'd like to contribute. But I'll be fashionably late getting there. Right now I'm bobbing around near Cassiar Island, and I haven't even had breakfast yet. And I've got to get hooked up at the airport."

I'm sure Rick can visualize me as I plod along. I've held him up with my slow process of getting ready to ride on a few occasions. On the other hand, you really can't hold Rick up for long. If you try, he simply speeds off in front of you, always quick to the destination.

"Maybe I'll see you there," says Rick.

But we both know I probably won't get there until all the trail building is complete.

* * * * *

ON MY WAY INTO TOWN, I drive through the parking lot at Quality Foods, looking for quads in the back of pickup trucks. This is where the Powell River ATV Club Wednesday Crew meets in the morning for coffee, before heading out to their day's targeted area for trail maintenance. They do everything from pruning local trails to building new paths into the backcountry. I've seen pictures – what they do is amazing. There seems to be no level of trail construction they can't handle. Theo needs it.

But there are no quads in trucks in the grocery store parking lot. Not surprising, since it's now pushing 10 o'clock, so they've already left. I'll be several hours behind them. Typically, they like to finish up quickly (which is realistic when you're as talented as they are), using the remainder of the day to ride and explore. Still, I'll give it a try. Maybe I can find them before they're finished trail building for the day.

I eat my breakfast without doddling, and I'm at the airport by 10:45. There's still plenty of daylight to make it into Theodosia and back, but the crew may be finished before I get there. In that case, I can be the first recreational rider to take advantage of their work. Hopefully, I'll be able to report back to Margy that this trail is now ready for her. It's optimistic thinking.

I hook up my truck to the quad trailer at the airport, and pull out of the open-ended hangar onto the taxiway to off-load Margy's quad, which sits on the back of the trailer. I've been known to haul both quads to my off-load location, leaving one on the trailer while I ride. That's the simple solution, but not the one acceptable to local riders. I'm far too trusting of those who pass by a trailer with a quad on it in the middle of nowhere. After all, I can lock it to the trailer, and lock the trailer to the truck. But it's not accepted local practice to leave a quad this way, and today my antics will be visible to the Wednesday Crew. So I take the time to unstrap Margy's quad and drive it off the trailer. Then I lock it to the big post in the hangar and head out the gate. It's one of the few times I've done this right while riding solo, but it consumes less time than I expect. Maybe I'll mend my ways in the future. Probably not.

One errand remains in town, since I might not get back until after the bookstore in the mall closes. So I find a big double parking space, and make a book delivery. Pulling into the mall with the trailer is more comfortable than it usually is. Through my rearview mirror, I can see out the back window of the truck (and through the truck's shell canopy window) better than normal. I conclude that having only one quad on the trailer makes for better rearward visibility, another reason to consider mending my ways. With the side mirrors to assist me, I navigate through the mall area without causing undo hazard to the clientele. But I need to keep reminding myself I'm towing a trailer, so I don't make the typical amateur mistake of forgetting the long trailer is there and cutting turns too close.

I deliver my books to the bookstore, and maneuver down to Highway 101, where the trailer seems to tow better than normal, probably because of the lighter weight with only one quad. That's even more reason to keep looking in the mirrors to remind me I'm towing something. John tells the story of towing a quad trailer up a hill on a remote logging road with his nephew, and then looking into his mirror to notice the quad was gone. He quickly turned around, and found the quad, which belonged to his nephew, sitting unharmed in the middle of the road a half kilometre behind him. He blamed his nephew for not properly tying the quad down, but together they shared a good laugh at their near-tragedy.

As I pull off the highway at Southview Road, I glance at my watch – approaching noon, and I haven't even off-loaded yet. When I reach my normally preferred (and always empty) off-load spot at a wide turnout with plenty of room for maneuvering, the area is full. Two trucks sit near the side of the road, and five more are in the wide area where I normally park – all with loading ramps down. This is the Wednesday Crew, that's for sure.

Theodosia Off-load – Wednesday Crew

The next turnout, which can comfortably hold two trucks, is also full. There might be room for my big trailer here, but I'll need to turn around to leave, and there's not much hope for such maneuvering at this location.

If I continue farther towards the spot I call the "stop sign in the wilderness," there's another large parking area before the sign, and then another farther beyond. Glancing in my rearview mirror, my quad is clear and distinct, riding well even though the road is now getting rough. So I continue another few kilometres, and find a big area with only one truck and plenty of room for me.

When I park and walk back to the trailer, I find the reason my rearview mirror is working so well today. The hinged window of the truck's shell canopy is wide open. Of course, this means it has been open since I left the airport, including during my excursion through the mall parking lot, along Highway 101, and all the way up Southview Road. It wasn't unsafe, but other motorists must have noticed, and it definitely was rather stupid. Then again, getting rid of the canopy's tinted window made visibility a lot better.

I off-load as quickly as possible, and I'm on my way, winding up the forest service road. I pass through the stop sign intersection, over the bridge, and eventually reach the end of the road where it turns into the trail winding down along Lancelot Inlet. Today the path is typically muddy, with big puddles and rocks that necessitate slowing down. There's one spot where a washout drops precipitously on both sides of the trail, but the Wednesday Crew's presence is obvious here, with a clear and safe path marked by fluorescent red marking tape.

This trail, like others in the wilderness, is ever changing. Today, for the first time I remember, the foliage on the trees is so diminished that the water of Lancelot Inlet is easily visible at several spots. A sparkling waterfall drops down towards me on the right side, where it splashes its way across the trail and then down towards Lancelot. I ride comfortably through this section, absorbing the beauty of the trail.

When I shift into four-wheel drive to start up the park-like path that's one of my favourites in this region, I notice the dirt at the entry of this trail has been recently built up into an even mound. The Wednesday Crew stopped here, too.

I wind my way through the impressive stand of trees, where newly cut logs lie off to the side, obviously rearranged today by those ahead of me. At the top of the hill, I exit the trees onto the logging road that leads to the final trail into Theodosia Valley, where most of the work is needed. This initial stretch of road is easy going. Through the trees, I look down to the narrow connection between Lancelot and Theosdosia Inlets. Then I come to the big rocks marking the beginning of the tough part of this route.

The first trench has smoothly manicured fresh dirt at the bottom, making the drop down and back up easy going. This was one of the worst spots in this section of the trail, and the main access problem here has been solved.

None of the crew nor their quads are visible yet, but the results of their work is everywhere. Big rocks have been removed from critical areas and placed in scenic locations or used as fill mixed with dirt in deep trenches. It's smooth going all the way, including a significant improvement in the last stretch of the trail as it drops down to the open area near the logging dock. I've always had trouble negotiating this lower section, but somehow it's smoother and easier today. I can't exactly determine how this portion has been improved, but it's definitely a better path now. The proof is in the riding.

When I make the final descent into the open area, a white pickup truck is positioned here, as it often is, off to the side of the road leading to Theodosia Valley. The implication is there's active logging ahead, and I'm not prepared to tackle the main alone. As I park along the cliff, out of the way of logging trucks, the supervisor in the white truck walks over to meet me.

"Beauty of a day, eh?" he says in a friendly voice.

"Sure is," I reply. "I bet there's been a lot of quad riders working on the trail today."

"I counted eleven of them. They left a while ago, headed up the main towards Rupert's Farm, I think."

Looking ahead, I see a hodgepodge of truck lights, congregated at the parking area near the middle of this very industrial logging assembly area.

"Lot of trucks today," I note.

"Business is good," he replies. "It's nice to be back to work."

Logging is one of the biggest on-and-off businesses of all time. There are booming times, and there are times when it seems trees will never fall again. This is definitely one of the booming times. The log pens in the bay are full, and a big yacht sits next to a crew boat at the dock.

"Looks like a private boat over there," I say. "Funny time of the year to see recreational boaters."

"It's private, but being rented out as a logging camp for some of the guys. Nice 50-footer."

A man is on the boat's upper deck, dressed more like a yacht captain than a logger, is hauling a satellite antenna up over the rail.

Theodosia Inlet

"Looks like he's going to have TV," I say.

"Sure. They have everything. Getting all set up for the Super Bowl this weekend."

Oh. I can envision it – rowdy loggers sitting around on a rented yacht watching the Super Bowl. I hope the captain has checked his insurance.

As for me, I'm pleased to see the entry trail to Theodosia in such good shape. I'll be one of the prime beneficiaries of their great work. Thanks, Wednesday Crew!

* * * * *

ONE OF OUR ATV CLUB'S BIGGEST PROJECTS involves the construction of a cabin at Elk Lake. This undertaking is particular noteworthy since it teams up local hikers with quad riders, two groups that haven't always seen eye-to-eye. Terry leads the charge for our club, along with the Wednesday Crew, and sends out an email announcement in September – there'll be a hot dog barbecue at the new cabin, in celebration of the project's completion. I want to support this accomplishment, and respond to Terry's message by saying: "I'll be there, unless it's pouring, of course."

The weather does look a bit chancy, with a forecast indicating 60 percent chance of rain. But I haven't ridden a quad in several months, and both the vehicle and my body could use the activity. I plan to ride somewhere, even if it turns out to be a shorter than the trip to Elk Lake, and I invite Doug to join me at Edgehill School parking lot at 9:30 am. From there, we'll ride to Duck Lake, where we'll join Terry and the others heading up Granite Main to Elk Lake.

"I'll be there tomorrow, if the weather's descent," says Doug. "I'll admit I'm pretty much a fair weather rider."

He's also a hard rider, but there's nothing wrong with enjoying it in the good weather.

"I plan to go anyway, unless it's pissin' down rain," I reply. "Invite Luke to come with us, if you'd like. I'll leave the Edgehill parking area at 9:45. If you're not there by then, I'll just go."

* * * * *

I SPEND A RESTLESS NIGHT in my condo in town, listening to the soothing sound of light rain, but unable to sleep. I often toss and turn when I try to sleep in town, probably because of the change from the ultimate quiet of the lake. With the window wide open for some cool September air, city noises are always in the background. Cars gun their engines as they occasionally pass by, turning to climb the hill, and even the clanging of sailboat tackle in the harbour below me is less than calming. Of course, a full Saturday of college football on TV hasn't helped. My eyes feel literally bugged out by the time I crawl into bed after the last battle for the goal line.

Besides, when a trip is coming up the next day, I tend to worry that I won't sleep, and end up tired before the journey begins. Tonight, I add concern for the weather to the mix. Worry – no sleep; no sleep – more worry. It's a self-fulfilling prophecy.

I arise early the next morning, determined to get a leisurely start. It always takes longer to get ready for a ride than I budget, and today I don't want to be rushed. There's the safety issue – haste adds to miscalculation, particularly when I'm as tired as I seem this morning.

But if I go slow, I'll not be a hazard to myself or anyone else. So I head for the airport at 8 o'clock, plenty of time to hook up to the trailer and be waiting for Doug when (if) he arrives at the Edgehill parking lot.

If I hadn't promised Doug I would be riding today, it's likely I would cancel my trip. The light rain from the dark morning sky would be enough of an excuse. Yet, I remind myself that once I get going, it'll be worth the effort. I often find I'm lackluster about doing things like this until I'm finally on my way. Then, almost always, I'm glad I didn't stay home.

Once I've hooked up the quad trailer at the airport, little extra time remains to make it to Edgehill by 9:30. When Margy is out of town, as she is now, I must accomplish the hookup by myself, and it usually takes noticeably longer. Since her silver quad is on the back of the trailer, I'll ride it today. Last on, first off. Plus, her bike has lower miles, so it'll be good to exercise it.

I lock the axle of my red quad to the trailer rail with a heavy chain and padlock, and double secure it with a cable and combo lock. I feel fine leaving the second quad in the Edgehill lot. To prevent the criticism other riders may throw my way, I usually try to avoid conversations about my apathy: "I always like to travel with a spare quad. You never know when you might need an extra starter or another cylinder."

That usually ends the conversation rather quickly, while my sparing partners try to decide if I'm serious. In truth, I take both quads because I'm lazy. It avoids an extra off-load when I depart and on-load when I return.

Pulling into the Edgehill lot, the light rain has stopped. Brian and Donna are off-loading their quad, and donning their rain gear.

"We need to go on ahead, rather than wait for you," says Donna. "We promised Terry we'd meet him at the Pit to help haul the food."

"You don't want to wait for me anyway," I reply. "It'll take me at least a half hour to get ready."

"Okay," says Donna. Her look indicates she's not sure whether I'm kidding. "We'll see you at the cabin then, since we won't be stopping at Duck Lake bridge, so we can get lunch set up for the rest of you guys."

"Shall I stop by the Pit to see if there's more to carry?" I ask.

I really don't know where the Pit is, but I assume it's the gravel pit on the main, after exiting the Edgehill trail system at the road to Duck Lake.

"Sure," says Brian. "I think we'll be okay, but you can stop to see if we need help. Terry bought lots of food."

"So where's the Pit?" I ask.

"Right around the corner to the left at the road," replies Brian.

"Oh, I thought it was to the right. I'll stop by."

But I think he really means to the right, although he definitely said "left." In any case, it's near the intersection, so I'll be able to find it.

As Brian and Donna drive their quad into the woods, I unstrap Margy's bike, let it warm up, and then off-load it from the trailer. I move equipment around, taking my helmet and gloves from my quad's rear box and putting them in the silver bike's box. Other trucks are arriving in the lot now, but nobody I recognize. Several of them have their quads out of their trucks before I'm ready to go. It doesn't take me a half hour, but it's close.

Edgehill School Parking

Doug still hasn't arrived, nor do I expect him to, considering the morning dreariness. I wait until a few minutes after 9:45, and then depart.

"Go slow, and pay attention" I say to myself, as I enter the forest. This will be worth repeating numerous times today. I feel wide-awake now, but my lack of sleep is still a hidden hazard that's worth my attention. There's no reason to hurry, and it's a wise cautionary self-notice. If I don't rush, I'll be fine.

The moment I enter the trail, the trees engulf me. The sun beams between the branches now. Today has turned out better weather-wise than expected, and I suddenly feel vibrant and pleased I'm here. So often it's that way. Once the engine is running, all is well. Two hours ago I was ready to cancel.

The short ride to the road is simple and lacking in challenge. Some of the trenches – a bit deep immediately after the winter – have been worn smooth, undoubtedly tended to by the Wednesday Crew. I make it a point to pay attention and go slow, but it's an easy trek to the main road.

At the intersection, I stop and glance at my watch – 10:10, plenty of time to check to see if all of the food has left the Pit. So is it to the right (as I remember it) or to the left (as Brian has mentioned)? I turn to the left, figuring I'll turn around if I don't encounter it immediately.

So I turn and ride awhile. No Pit.

I ride a little farther, and pull off to the side of the road, trying to decide whether to continue or turn around. As I sit pondering the situation, two quads speed past, headed for Duck Lake. I wave; they wave. Now another quad appears, headed the same way. More waves. Was that Brian and Donna?

I check my watch – 10:20, and the meeting at the bridge is supposedly 10:30. But I've promised Brian and Donna I'll check for any help needed at the Pit. Or did they just pass me?

I turn back towards Duck Lake Bridge. After passing the Edgehill exit point on the road, I ride on far enough to know the Pit isn't in this direction. So I simply hadn't ridden far enough to find it the other way. Basically, I'm lost before I even begin. But at least I'm riding slow and careful.

At the bridge, only one quad sits in the area where I expected to find lots of quads. Don is driving and Jim (a hiker) is doubling behind him. Jim is a volunteer carpenter, one of the key people for the Elk Cabin plan, designing and organizing the materials and directing the project from the very beginning.

"Bunch of bikes just went by, headed up to the cabin," says Don. "Here come some more."

Around the corner, headed towards us are a line of three quads, followed soon thereafter by two more. Terry leads the pack, and he parks next to me. More than the normal number of women are involved in today's celebration, some regular riders with our club and others along to support the cabin-building accomplishments of their husbands.

When helmets are finally off, I recognize a few people I know, including Mario.

"I hear the Wednesday Crew built a little cabin," I say to Mario.

"Even bigger than little," he replies.

"I saw the photos," I say. "Quite an accomplishment."

"So I see you're riding your wife's trusty steed today," says Mario.

"Need to put some miles on it."

"Sure, sure. Good excuse."

We wait until 10:30, and then we're off. We follow Duck Lake Branch 3 past Mud Lake to the Granite Lake junction. Turning left, we begin the climb on one of the region's most scenic mains. I've always liked this trail, partly because it was one of my first off-road adventures. The dangerously deep trenches I remember from years past have blended into much easier traveling now. Some of this is undoubtedly because of the work of the Wednesday Crew. But I'm sure most of it is because of the distortion of memory in the face of experience. I may not be an advanced rider, but I certainly have come a long way.

When the granite base becomes more imposing, I stop and shift into four-wheel drive. Although I probably won't need it during this climb, I'm not sure what lies ahead. My experience may have muted some of the danger, but four-wheel drive makes climbing out of the small trenches easier, and there's no need to go fast here. In front of me is a line of four quads led by Terry, with two more behind me.

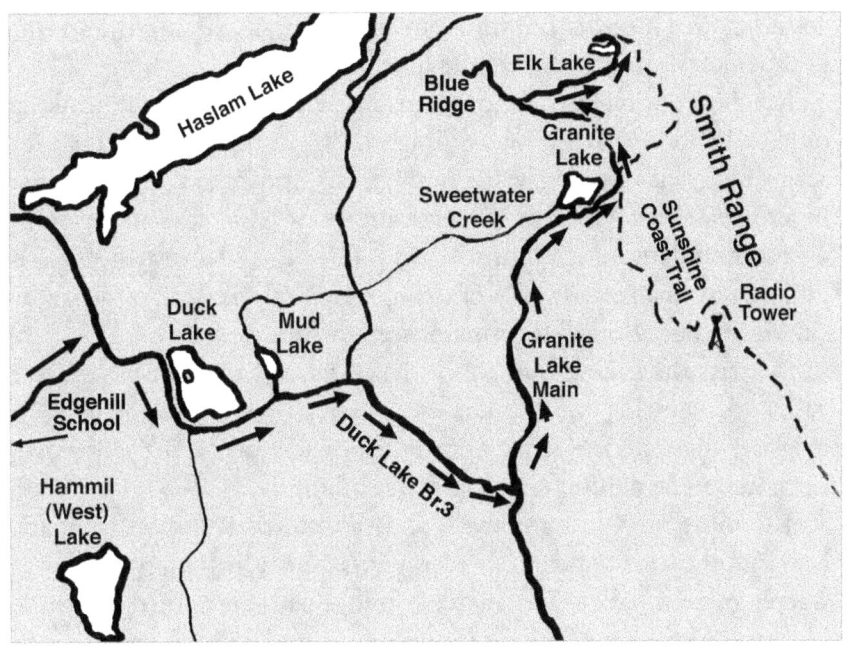

Edgehill to Elk Lake

Just before the biggest trench (once barely at my operational limit), we stop where a truck is parked off to the side of the trail, just as Terry told us to expect. We pick up two hikers headed to the cabin celebration. One of the hikers doubles behind Mario, and the other behind another rider. I follow Mario, watching him explain what I imagine to be "quad stuff "to the hiker as we proceed. This mix of bikers and hikers is a healthy one, a long-needed improvement in our local area. The cabin project has brought the two groups together to share enormous patches of common ground.

We pass the turnoff to Granite Lake, a spot I'll visit on my way back down. This lake has special memories for me, and I'll want to try to catch one of the lake's unusual charcoal-gray trout, and just sit and look at the beautiful tranquil surroundings.

As we approach the wooden bridge across the stream above Granite Lake, I stop to let Mario get completely across first. It's best to allow only one bike on a questionable bridge at a time, just in case the structure has hidden weaknesses. As Mario's quad passes over the creek, I notice his rider pointing out something farther up the stream. It's the hiker's turn to educate the biker.

Much of our region's famous Sunshine Coast Trail, a major hiking route, coincides with sections of quad trails. In these shared areas (as at Elk Lake), it's necessary for both hikers and bikers to remember the other's needs. We're finally building both ATV and hiking trails to accommodate both groups of people. Rather than saying "Keep Out!" we're finally saying: "Let's cooperate and get extra synergy by combining our efforts." It's a major step forward.

We pass the hiking trail to Elk Lake, part of the Sunshine Coast Trail, and then ride another klick to the quad turnoff to the lake. In this case, the trails are kept separate, so quad riders don't jeopardize the more serene nature of the narrower hiking trail.

The route in is well groomed, and easy to travel. As we approach the lake, the trees open to wider views, including marshes and a sweeping gentle valley. Nearing the cabin, quads are parked off to the side, keeping the trail clear for those coming and going. I find an open area holding several quads, with room for one more. It's necessary to back up a short incline to tuck myself into parking position.

After a short walk farther down the trail, the cabin and adjacent lake spring into view. The Wednesday Crew and the local hikers have outdone themselves!

With a nearly all-glass front facing towards the lake and an open structure on the opposite side, the picturesque cabin stands ready for visitors hiking along the Sunshine Coast Trail or arriving via quad or off-road motorcycle. Today the cabin's lower floor is full of people and food. In the upstairs loft, a vast empty sleeping area awaits future overnight visitors.

I walk down to the dock to take a picture of the cabin from below. A thin fog hugs Elk Lake, and a light sprinkle is in the air. But the weather seems close to perfect to me. And it's nice to have a roof over our head for our lunch today.

I linger on the dock, until there's a commotion up by the cabin, as a final pair of quads joins our group. It's Doug and Luke, better late than never.

Doug sees me on the dock, and walks down to join me.

"Glad to see you finally woke up this morning," I kid.

"Wasn't sure what the weather was going to do," Doug replies. "Then the sun came out, and I called Luke."

"This would be a good place to build a cabin for guys like us on a day like today," I say suggest.

"Yes, perfect," he replies.

When it's time to leave, Doug, Luke, and I divert farther up the mountain to the outlook at Blue Ridge, enjoying some more challenging riding together before we go home. It's all a reminder that weather changes quick around here, those who love exploring the wilderness by any mode of transportation can get along, and we often all end up in the same place. It's an important lesson.

Elk Lake Cabin

◊ ◊ ◊ ◊ ◊ ◊ ◊

Center-of-Book Photos

Museum Main, Chippewa Bay

Steam Donkey on Museum Main

Olsen's Lake

Looking down on Powell Lake from Heather Main

Heather Main above Chippewa Bay

Bro dressed for a cold ride

Chapter 7

Home Base

Heather Main and Hole in the Wall, Powell Lake

AT THE AIRPORT, Margy backs the truck up to our quad trailer, while I act as spotter. The truck slides effortlessly into place, and I give her the halt sign, right in front of the trailer hitch.

We go through our established routine, each of us doing our part to hook up the trailer. Margy inserts the tow bar into the truck, and clicks the safety pin in place, while I retrieve the electrical adapter from the truck's cab, and install it just below the rear bumper. Margy unlocks the chain securing the trailer and its quads to the hangar wall beam, and I pull the chocks, unhook the trailer's pintle hook, and unlatch the clasp. Together we nudge the trailer's hitch forward and over the ball. I lean on the trailer to keep the ball properly positioned while Margy cranks the hitch down. The final test is whether the clasp properly closes, since it'll completely latch only if the hitch is fully seated on the ball. Since the clasp is now streamlined, I assume the latch is locked. (Yes, I'm often a victim of the "assuming syndrome.") The pintle hook slides in smoothly; another indicator the latch is secure. I wind the crank until the trailer's support wheel is off the ground, and swing the bar horizontal until it snaps into travelling position. Done!

Margy pulls forward in the truck, while I call out the lights: "Left blinker, now right. Try the brakes." As often happens, I need to wiggle the electrical connector to get all the lights operating properly, but that's the result of minor corrosion from sitting year-round in the open-ended hangar. A quick jiggle solves the problem with the right blinker, and all is well.

We're off! Margy drives, while I ride shotgun, stopping briefly as we leave the airport so I can I unlock the gate, and relock it after our truck and trailer are through. We drive north on Highway 101, turning inland at Southview Road.

This is a historic (to us) day. We're taking our quads into Theodosia, up Heather Main, and all the way to Hole in the Wall, where we plan to leave them for several months. Riding our quads this season will be more efficient. By positioning our bikes near our cabin in Hole in the Wall, we should be able to ride more regularly without sacrificing a whole day away from the lake. We'll only need to take a short trip in our tin boat to get to the quads, carrying gas cans and riding gear, and we should be on our way in just a few minutes rather than a few hours. In theory, this is the ultimate solution for our summer riding dilemma, and there's lots for Margy and me to explore near Chippewa Bay, all easily reached on old logging roads.

But today will be a bit complicated. We'll first need to position our quads at Hole in the Wall, and then travel back down the lake by boat. At the Shinglemill Marina, we'll retrieve our truck at its off-load location (which, of course, requires a second vehicle), and then return the trailer to the airport hangar. Finally, we'll travel back up the lake, an itinerary that includes all the typical actions associated with our off-the-grid lifestyle – what we call the "complicated simple life."

* * * * *

ARRIVING AT OUR FAVOURITE PARKING SPOT on Southview Road, we go through our off-load routine. Again, each of us has things we normally do to speed the process (although our pace can't properly be called "speedy). Margy turns on the fuel valves for both quads (recently added to our personal checklist, for obvious reasons) and checks the oil levels. I lower the metal ramps and begin unstrapping the quads.

Margy climbs onto her quad, starts the engine, and lets it warm up. Then she slowly backs off the trailer. All is normal.

Now it's my turn. As I back up from my forward position on the trailer and start down the metal ramps, I experience a strange sensation. The back of the trailer is slowly tilting downward, but it's too late to switch gears and drive back onto the trailer. It's obvious what's happening, but there's no way to stop it, except to get off the trailer as quick as possible. I give the throttle an extra spurt in reverse as I roll off the tilting trailer. I watch the front tongue of the trailer swing upward, since (obvious now) it isn't attached to the truck!

Bam! The back of the trailer hits the ground, but I'm off now, so the whole process repeats itself in reverse. With the weight of my quad removed, the front of the trailer crashes down onto the truck's tow bar. *Bam!* again.

I shutdown my quad, and walk forward to survey the damage. Margy's already there, inspecting the trailer's hitch that now rests awkwardly on the truck's tow bar at a slight angle, amazingly close to where it should be.

"Nice job, eh?" I say matter-of-factly.

"Yup. Next time let's latch the ball," replies Margy.

There's no damage, but we've been very fortunate. Obviously, when we lowered the hitch at the hangar, it hung up and didn't capture the ball. The latch was easily clipped shut, but that's because the hitch was riding on top of the ball and not attached at all. Securing the pintle hook did nothing but lock an unhooked hitch. As we rode along the highway, the hitch was precariously balanced on the ball. It's amazing it didn't pop off, which would have been even more memorable!

"The truck did seem to handle a bit funny in the turns," says Margy. "Must have been sliding around on the ball."

"We're lucky it was sliding rather than popping off," I say. "Even with the safety chains, it could have been a wild ride."

Lesson to be learned – after closing the clasp and securing the pintle hook, give one final upward pull on the trailer's hitch to see if it's really attached. This trailer is light enough that an unattached ball would be obvious during such a test. You won't catch us making the same mistake again. (Instead, we'll make some other mistake.)

After all of this unexpected excitement, we're finally ready to ride. When you've dodged fate as we have today, it's appropriate to be grateful.

* * * * *

TODAY'S RIDE IS TYPICALLY ENJOYABLE, a scenic trip down the rocky trail towards Lancelot Inlet, then up through the park-like trail leading to the Theodosia logging dock. However, I'm a bit concerned about the final drop into Theodosia Inlet, since this trail has deteriorated again in recent months. Based on condition reports from John, I'm not sure Margy will be able to negotiate the final section of the trail. I expect I'll need to ferry her bike through this short stretch while she walks the route.

When we reach the predicted difficult portion of the trail, it's worse than I expect. Right away, I can see that entering this part of the trail will require careful maneuvering across a precarious looking bridge constructed of small logs joined together across a major trench. What's beyond, I'm not sure, but I know Margy isn't going to like this. Margy doesn't deserve uncomfortable, and I feel bad about forcing this ride today. Fortunately, we've become adaptable to changes in our plans, a flexibility that's developed over the years as we've become engaged in our complicated simple life. Living off the grid in this beautiful region has caused changes for the better.

"Doesn't look so great, does it?" I note.

"Not at all," Margy replies. "I won't be able to do it."

"And you don't have to do it. Don't have to walk it either. We can turn around and take a leisurely ride back to the truck. There's plenty of sunlight left, so we can still get back up the lake before dark."

"Sounds good to me," she answers, with a broad grin on her face.

We just love a chance to go up the lake, by quad or boat. Rather than this being a failure, today is a rousing success. There'll be other days to bring the quads into Hole in the Wall, and John will be glad to help us.

*****

YES, THERE ARE OTHER OPPORTUNITIES to bring our quads to Hole in the Wall, but they slip away. We spend the summer as we always have – travelling down the lake for our quad rides. One thing happens, and then another, and pretty soon winter snow (in autumn) moves into the high country. Heather Main, the high trail connecting Theodosia with Powell Lake's Chippewa Bay, will be impassible until late spring or early summer, so it'll be next year before we can transfer our quads.

The following spring, Heather Main becomes passible earlier than expected due to a mild winter. John rode through last week, encountering only minor snow banks that didn't hinder his progress. But John isn't sure about the alternate (and shorter) route over the Bunsters he wants to attempt with me. The Last Chance Trail is challenging in the best of conditions. During the spring, it keeps its snow-cover longer than Heather Main, even though it's a slightly lower elevation. A dense canopy of trees along an extended section of the Last Chance Trail tends to delay snow-melt well into summer. No one has ridden this route this year, which is exactly why John wants to try it.

* * * * *

WHEN MY ALARM GOES OFF AT 6:45 AM, Margy wakes up with me, and immediately comments: "It's windy."

"Clearing winds," I reply.

"Sometimes they're the worse."

I'm focused on today's plans with John, which often causes me to justify what shouldn't be justified. Margy is referring to our self-imposed wind limits for travelling on the lake, and she's right about clearing winds – they can be the strongest of all.

I phone John, and we discuss Plan B.

"I'll wait for the wind to go down before I leave," I say. "Should still be at your house by 11 o'clock, if that will work for you."

"Got another project I can work on," replies John, which makes me feel better. "Don has a 15-horse outboard he wants me to fix, so I need to do some troubleshooting."

"Good. I'll call you when I get to town."

By mid-morning, the wind is substantially reduced, but now it's starting to rain. The forecast is for clearing today, although weather forecasts change fast around here. But the reduced wind means its safe to depart the cabin.

I drive the tin boat into the back of the Hole, holding an umbrella to keep from getting drenched, and Margy meets me there with the Campion. The tin boat will be our transportation back to my cabin when John and I arrive with the quads.

Now it's down the lake in the Campion for Margy and me. I phone John when I arrive at the Shinglemill, and then drop Margy at the condo, where she has some Internet projects. Then I drive to the airport, and hook up to the quad trailer, carrying our two quads.

When I arrive at John's house, he's taken the engine cover off his friend's two-stroke outboard motor, and is making adjustments while it's running in a big barrel, splashing water out onto the grass.

"Trying to fix this for Don," says John over the noise of the running engine. "It's the carburetor, but now it's running hot besides."

"No water from the pump," I say, noticing the absence of the normal stream that's supposed to pour out from the top of the leg.

"Can't run it for long," he says, carefully tapping one of the cylinders to check whether it's getting too hot. "Give me a hand moving it to the vise."

He shuts the engine down, and we haul the motor to the carport, where the big vise awaits. A hefty cross-board is already in place to receive the leg.

"I'll need to drop the gear case," he says. "But we'll leave it for now. Let's go."

In just a few minutes, we're on our way, driving both of our trucks to the Shinglemill – the complicated simple life in action again. We'll use my truck to tow the trailer with the two quads to the off-load site. With John's truck left at the Shinglemill, we'll have transportation after we come back down the lake later today. The already prepositioned tin boat at Hole in the Wall will be needed to get back to my cabin when we arrive with the quads. It'll take another boat to bring us down the lake (since the Campion is already at the Shinglemill), and then we'll use John's truck to retrieve my truck at the quad off-load location on Southview Road. I'll drive back to the condo to pickup Margy, drop the trailer at the airport hangar, and the two of us will ferry both boats back to the cabin. It's amazing how intricate our waterland transportation plans can become, but we love working out the logistics. How many trucks, boats, trailers, and quads will it take to accomplish today's mission? Answer: a lot. (Eight, to be exact.)

* * * * *

AT SOUTHVIEW ROAD, we off-load the two quads and are quickly on our way. We drive north to the stop sign in the middle of nowhere, and turn right to begin our climb into the Bunster Range. We make a brief stop at the lookout over Okeover Inlet, and then start up Theodosia Branch 2. We cross Appleton Creek twice as it meanders towards the sea, and then take the turnoff towards the Last Chance Trail.

John leads the entire way, driving Margy's quad, while I follow close behind. Seldom does he ride without Bro, but there's no dog carrier box on Margy's quad, so this is a rare outing when John can drive faster than normal. As I try to keep up, it's obvious he's taking advantage of the situation by keeping up a fast pace. It's safe, but I don't find any time to relax and enjoy the passing scenery until John stops for a family of grouse that are leisurely crossing the road.

A few minutes later, now on the Last Chance Trail, we see our first snow. At first, it's only a few patches off to the side of the trail in the low spots, but soon it's covering the trail in a complete white blanket. It's mushy, old snow, but that's even worse for traction. The biggest problem, however, involves places where the depth of the snow exceeds a foot. Without adequate ground clearance for our undercarriage, regardless of traction, we're quickly bogged down.

"Lockers!" yells John, as we approach an extended snowy stretch under a thick canopy of trees. This is one of the cedar groves that blocks the sunlight, prolonging the groundcover of snow until summer.

Last Chance Trail

I search for the differential lockers switch, and finally find the moveable cover that allows me to access the button. I watch John start up a snowy, precipitous climbing curve that looks well beyond our abilities today.

Mud flies as John's tires try to dig in, but the depth of the snow is too much. Pretty soon he's stuck, and I'm stopped a short distance back. John walks down to my quad, and the two of us rock my bike to give me enough traction to back out of the muddy mess. Then we tackle John's quad, and finally extract it back down the hill to better conditions.

We walk the trail further uphill to get a better look, hoping the next slope will be gentler, even though we still haven't found a way through this first seemingly-impossible section. The snow only gets thicker. As we walk back to our bikes, John says he's willing to give up on this trail for today, which is a bit of surprise. Usually, he'll work at a tough spot over and over, regardless of how many times he gets stuck. But today he's worried about the waning daylight hours.

"We still have time to backtrack and take the Theo route," he says. "But we'll have to hurry to make it through before dark?"

What started out as a fairly leisurely ride (by John's standards) will now become a race. I've been involved in races with John before, and they're notoriously – in a word – "fast!"

I manage to keep up with him on the way back down the Last Chance Trail, but it takes my total concentration on the path, bouncing every which way. When we reach Theodosia Branch 2, it's a major rush down the road to the stop sign in the middle of nowhere, where we turn right and head into Theodosia Valley. Going very fast, of course.

The logs that form the bridge entryway into Theodosia are not as bad as I expected, remembering when Margy and I turned back at this spot last summer. It looks like the Wednesday Crew has been here again. There's a trench just beyond the bridge that's quite precarious, but then we're down and out of the worst of it, with my quad seeming to spit out of the mud at the logging dock.

We pull off at the parking area near the dock, where a crew boat is about to depart. I think we may finally be stopping for a rest, but John yells down to the captain of the boat, who is about to step aboard.

"Are they still haulin'?" hollers John.

"Nothing past the water tank!" the captain yells back. Then he hops aboard his boat, engine already running, and immediately pulls away.

"Should be okay," says John. "We'll go slow until the tank. Be ready to drive into the ditch if we see any logging trucks before we get there."

Today is a weekday, so logging is in progress. Fortunately, it's the end of the workday, so all of the trucks are shutting down, except for a few joining the main road between here and the water tank.

In less than a klick, the water tank appears on our left at an intersection, while a spur to the right holds a few parked logging trucks. Once safely past this spot, we shouldn't face any oncoming traffic.

We make one more stop at the log sort, a few klicks up the road where Theodosia Main joins Heather Main. There we eat our long delayed lunch, which is now dinner. John can really slow down (suddenly) when it involves food, so I savour such moments.

Then we're on our way again, riding through the extensive logging slash that finally leads to the uphill climb on Heather Main. We pass the spot where I snapped the snowshoe photo for the cover of *Up the Winter Trail*, a location now barely distinguishable in the late spring scenery. It seems like a completely different place with the passage of seasons. In fact, it is.

High on Heather Main, I follow John through the final kilometres of today's this-way, no-that-way journey. He rides fast, and I tuck in close behind. Soon we're at the junction with the JR Cutoff, the trail leading down to Chippewa Bay, where John and I (and Bro) were up close and personal with a cougar less than two weeks ago (*Off the Grid*, Chapter 17). As we descend through the forest on the JR Cutoff (named after John and his brother, Rick, who blazed this trail), I scan through the thick grove of trees. There's no doubt that the cougar is still here, protecting his territory, probably watching us right now.

When we break out into the logging slash at the bottom of the trail, I relax a bit, no longer feeling like cougar bait. We rejoin the lower reaches of Heather Main, dropping down towards Chippewa Bay.

It's downhill the rest of the way, and we've clearly beaten darkness. John slows a bit, and we ride almost leisurely through our descent to Powell Lake. I catch a glimpse of the tranquil water and the floating cabins north of First Narrows. It's a reassuring sight. We're home.

Quads at Hole in Wall

Chapter 8

Mechanic without a Toolbox
Chippewa Bay, Powell Lake

It's almost as much my fault as John's. I encourage him every step of the way. He's been thinking about buying a side-by-side off-road two-seater for some time, and when a reasonably priced Suzuki Samurai comes up for sale, he buys it. Actually, this vehicle is the successor to the Samurai, one of the original SUVs of the world, a vehicle that received a lot of bad press in its day. The Samurai had a high center of gravity and a tight turning radius, resulting in routine rollovers that grabbed the headlines. John's new (old) four-wheel drive model is the next-of-the-line Suzuki, equipped with a skookum roll bar and a geared-down turning radius that makes tight turns difficult, often necessitating a series of reverse-then-forward maneuvers to come around a corner.

But the price is right. Of course, it needs lots of work. On the other hand, John is used to work, so he tackles the repairs immediately, and soon the vehicle is running smoothly. That is, it runs well when it runs, but it has a habit of not running very long before something bad happens. The small engine literally purrs like a low-horsepower sewing machine. The engine compartment includes a lot of lose wires dead-ending before they reach the radio, heater, and other normally essential functions. But it looks sporty. We refer to it as the "Jeep."

Getting it to a place to ride, since it's not highway licenced, is a challenge. Unlike John's quad, it won't fit in the back of his truck, so he has to trailer it to an off-load location, and then play with the wires under the hood to get it running.

One weekend, John brings the Jeep all the way into Chippewa Bay, a long trek through Theodosia Valley and up (and then down) Heather Main. There's no secure place to park, but we've carved out a temporary spot for my quads close to Hole in the Wall, with water access by tin boat, and it'll work fine for the Jeep, too.

John's drive into Chippewa Bay in the Jeep is important to both of us. He's promised to help me prune the trail for our quads so Margy and I can get in and out easier. After you leave Chippewa Bay, the route to our temporary parking area is an overgrown logging road that needs lots of work to make it easily passible. The next few days with the Jeep will be a mix of accessing areas we don't normally explore and getting some trail work done at the same time.

* * * * *

JOHN'S TRIP INTO CHIPPEWA BAY goes almost without incident. Of course, every trip in the Jeep is an adventure, often including mechanical failures that tax John's ingenuity. For him, that's part of the fun. Not that engine problems on Heather Main are something to look forward to, but after a hard day's drive (and only two stops for repairs), he's parked near Hole in the Wall.

The next day, John, Margy, Bro, and I cram ourselves into the tin boat for a short trip to our makeshift parking area. Once ashore, we slug our way through the bushes, and end up in the cramped area containing our vehicles. John hops aboard the Jeep, and the small battery cranks the starter admirably with an encouraging *uhh-uhh-uhh*, but there's no *vroom-vroom-vroom*. The Jeep won't start.

"Doesn't sound right," says John. "Lots of crankin' power, but no ignition."

"Could it be flooded?" I ask.

"Maybe, but I don't think so."

John's mechanical abilities far exceed mine, so much so that I used to be afraid to suggest anything in situations like this. But I've learned John has an unusual attitude for someone so mechanically inclined. He listens to suggestions from others, even mechanical idiots like me. John is quick to accept any input for his constantly whirling repairman's brain. Sometimes my crude ideas actually work. Typically, John will appear to ignore anything mechanical I might offer, but I know he's always paying attention. In some cases, he returns to my ideas later, incorporating them with his own inventiveness to fix an ailing engine.

John tries a flooded start, pushing the throttle to the floor and holding it there while he moves the manual choke lever to the closed position. He cranks again. More *uhh-uhh-uhh*, but still no *vroom-vroom-vroom*.

"Good battery," I say.

This battery hasn't always performed so well, but today it seems fully charged and working like mad. It won't last long.

"Let's take a look at the carburetor," says John. "I don't think it's getting any fuel."

He pops the hood and plays with the carburetor. We've brought along a gas can, so we pour some fuel into the plastic cap of an oil bottle, and tip it into the venturi-shaped throat as primer. Another attempted start, with the same disturbing results. The engine doesn't fire, and the small battery now exhibits deteriorating cranking power.

"Could it be out of gas?" asks Margy.

I expect an immediate "No!" Instead, John rubs his fingers on his chin and thinks it through. Margy has even less mechanical ability than I do, but John considers everybody's input.

"Should be plenty of gas," he says. "But the fuel gauge is crap. So go ahead and put some in."

I unscrew the cap from the gas can, and add some fuel. After pouring only a few litres, the tank overflows, catching me by surprise. Gas pours over the fender and down onto my foot.

"It's nearly full!" I yell to John, who is back in the driver's seat, ready to try again.

"I thought so," says John. "I added some gas on Heather Main. So it's got to be getting gas."

"Unless your tank is full of water," I reply. "Somebody could've stolen all your gas and filled your tank with water."

Ridiculous, of course, but I like to kid John about his Jeep. Parked here at Hole in the Wall, even temporarily, he's worried about security. Of course, since I'm a full-time resident, I watch any visitors like a hawk. But here, in only two days, John is already suspicious.

"I don't think anyone has been here since yesterday," says John. "Could be the spark plugs. If I had a plug wrench, we could see if they're dry. If I flooded the engine, the plugs could be soaked with gas."

John usually doesn't go anywhere without a toolbox, and he's brought a big one today. Everything, of course, except a plug wrench. (On the other hand, I've seen John purposefully refuse to take even a pair of pliers with him, as he sometimes does with the Jeep, even though it wins the award as his most unreliable machine. There's something about tempting fate that makes John happy.)

"Let's try a bigger battery," he says. "We can remove the one from the tin boat, and it'll crank the engine a lot faster. Might be enough to do the trick."

"Okay," I say. "But it's a pretty sorry day when my tin boat's battery is more powerful than the battery in your Jeep."

Once John focuses on a project, he never gives up. We could be here all day. We'll use every bit of innovation (and every available electron) to try to solve this problem, so Margy and I might as well settle in.

While John trudges back through the bush to the tin boat, I rummage through his toolbox, looking for a spark plug wrench. I find a plug wrench for a chainsaw, but it probably won't fit.

"I found this," I tell John when he returns with the battery from the boat.

I hand him the wrench, and he tries to maneuver it into position. As expected, it doesn't fit the plug. Then John replaces the battery and tries again. This time the engine rotates faster. There's a brief firing of the engine, but it doesn't catch.

"Close!" says John. "Let's try some more fuel in the carburetor."

We go through the whole process again, pouring fuel into the plastic cap and dumping it into the carburetor. While we're under the hood, I point to the stopgap air filter, an old sock wrapped around the intake port.

"Could it be lack of air?" I ask.

Again, John listens to my suggestion, pulling the sock off the intake. Even with the more powerful battery, the cap-full of fuel, and the removed sock, the engine still refuses to start.

We pull the line off the fuel pump, and John cranks the engine while I watch gas spurting out, proving the pump is operating properly. We try everything John, Margy, and I can think of. We even ask Bro.

"Bro, what do you think?" I ask.

Woof!

Just as we (even John) are about to give up, the engine starts. It doesn't ignite smoothly, but John keeps the motor running until lots of rough coughing finally smooths out. In a few minutes, he shuts off the engine and tries starting it again. It fires normally and starts immediately. After two more test starts, including one with the original Jeep battery, we get ready to go. But we don't know what caused the problem, so we shouldn't go far today.

* * * * *

MARGY RIDES UP FRONT WITH JOHN, while Bro and I squeeze ourselves into the back of the Jeep. There are no seats here, but I try to make myself comfortable with an old boat cushion, and prop my feet forward near the gearshift handle between John and Margy. We bounce our way up the make-do trail to the old logging road.

Jammed in back with Bro, I sit higher than the front seat, looking out over the roll bar. Except for the bite of the cold air flowing past, I should be quite comfortable, and it gives Bro plenty of room to stretch out at my feet.

As I try to find a comfortable position, I reach in my pocket for my heavy gloves, but find nothing. When I saw how cold it was today, I switched jackets back at the cabin, and I forgot to grab my gloves. In addition to this major omission, I'm fighting with the zipper for my jacket. No matter how hard I try, the zipper won't budge. I give up, and use the jacket's Velcro strap that serves almost as well. But as the Jeep bounces along the narrow trail, the strap keeps popping open. If I don't solve these problems, it's going to be a very cold day riding back here.

I open my backpack, which is propped next to me, and fumble around inside until I feel the extra pair of socks I carry with me almost everywhere (wet feet are one of the worst curses I can imagine). They're heavy wool, which will be appreciated if my feet get wet, but now they have a more important purpose. I pull the socks over my hands as improvised mittens, grab the cold metal roll bar, and am finally secure in the rocking vehicle. My hands look a little funny, but it works for me.

We pop out of the rough trail through a final tight corner, onto a better (still not good) old logging road. The turn causes the vehicle to lean precariously to the right. We all lean to the left to counteract the roll. I look over at Bro, and even he is leaning sideways.

For the rest of the trip to Chippewa Bay, I ride half-sitting and half-standing, sock-covered hands on the roll bar and a big dog at my feet. Bro and I bounce every which way. Margy and John bump around nearly as much in their plush (by comparison) bucket seats.

Now on a slightly wider road, we continue around the periphery of Chippewa Bay, stopping occasionally to trim alder branches projecting over the old road. We leave most of the new growth that juts upward from the center of the trail. It's tall, but no major hindrance for the Jeep. John says it won't stop a quad either. By the end of the day, we've come a long ways in upgrading the path our quads will take regularly during the next few months.

Cutting fallen tree

A fallen tree pops into view. John was able to maneuver around (or over) it on his way down from Heather Main yesterday, but I'm not sure how. Now he attacks it with his chain saw, cutting the section that's fallen across the road into two big pieces. Once we've hauled the chunks to the side, the road is wide enough for the Jeep to pass, and it'll make the going a lot better for our quads as well.

Within a few hundred metres, another fallen tree requires the same treatment. It's stop-and-go for the next few kilometres as we cut our way towards the Chippewa Bay logging dock, improving the trail just as I'd hoped.

John veers to the left to go around a big branch that partially blocks our path, and we all lean in the opposite direction. *Bam!* – sounds like a backfire to me. John pulls to an immediate stop.

"Blew a tire," John says disgustedly.

What we find is worse than bad. The sidewall of a rear tire has been punctured by a cutoff trunk hidden in the rut at the side of the road. The tire has plenty of tread-life left, but the damage won't be reparable. Fortunately, we're carrying a spare, along with the tire change kit it.

Jeep tire change

We've traveled only a short distance and already have a flat tire. And the engine-starting problem remains fresh in my mind, so I'm wondering if we should simply turn around and go back. Of course, John accepts no such concept. Once he plans to go riding, he's going riding, regardless of obstacles.

We work together to change the tire. In just a few minutes we're on our way again. But I wonder if the Jeep's engine will let us down as we get farther from home. It's the kind of lesson this finicky vehicle might try to teach us.

When we stop for lunch at the Chippewa Bay logging dock, I hope the engine will restart. We could hike back from here, although it would be a very long walk. But I settle down and enjoy the break. John and I climb down to an old logging raft and then wander along the shore. Margy remains near the Jeep, exploring along the sides of the road. I glance back and see her shooting pictures of roadside flowers with her camera.

When it's time to crank the engine, I hold my breath, but it starts flawlessly, and we head back towards the cabin. Our first attempt

Jeep at Chippewa Bay

at improving the trail for future quad rides has been a big success. And we'll make it back to Hole in Wall just fine, without any further mechanical problems. But this Jeep is a machine I can't decide whether to love or hate.

*****

JOHN IS WILLING TO WORK WITH ME on the trail one more day. Then he'll need to take the Jeep back to town. I'm quick to take advantage of his offer to meet the next morning for another trip through the still-marginal trail. When John shows up in his boat, ready to tackle the job, I try not to keep him waiting. I'm still eating breakfast, and haven't dressed for the trip yet. Margy will stay behind today, so she helps by quickly packing a lunch for me, while I gulp down the rest of my breakfast.

"I'll be ready in just a few minutes," I say.

"No problem," replies John. But I know it is.

John sits on the other side of the picnic table, rubbing down Bro, and acting like he's patient. He isn't. But I refuse to rush any faster. Things go best when I go slow enough to fully prepare for a ride like this. Today it includes putting on my hiking boots, which means lots of laces. No matter how I might try, I couldn't prepare fast enough for the always-ready-to-go John.

"Shall I bring my chainsaw?" I ask.

"Sure. That would help," replies John.

Of course, the saw isn't gassed up, so I add refueling to my mental list of preparations, as I re-lace my boots after missing an eyelet that leaves my sock doubled-over and jammed inside my shoe.

"How about tools?" I ask. "Anything we need?"

"I didn't bring them, but we shouldn't need any."

Am I riding in the same Jeep he is?

"I can bring whatever you need," I say.

"Okay, how about a pair of regular pliers and maybe a few plastic ties. Might need them for the air filter." (Which means the old sock that serves as a filter.)

"Sure," I reply. "How about my tool bag. I can bring it along."

"Don't need it," says John.

It's obviously one of those days when he wants to tempt fate.

"Okay. Are you sure there's nothing else you want me to bring?"

"Do you have some snipper pliers, in case we have to cut some wires?"

"Something like these," I say, pulling a pair of fishing pliers from my tool bag.

"Kinda' small, but they'll do," he says. "Just put the tools in your lunch bag, in case we need them."

There's not going to much Jeep maintenance today. Two pairs of pliers and a few plastic tires won't allow much of an engine overhaul.

* * * * *

WHEN JOHN, BRO, AND I ARRIVE AT THE JEEP, John climbs aboard immediately and cranks the starter. No surprise – the engine rotates smoothly, but fails to start.

John hops out, and pops the hood. I keep quiet, loading the chainsaw, lunch bag, and my pruning shears in the back of the vehicle.

John looks around the engine compartment, and starts twiddling with the loose wires that dead-end everywhere. After I've given him a

Engine compartment

few minutes to consider the situation, I come around to the front of the Jeep and gaze down at the small engine.

"Maybe you're out of windshield wiper fluid," I joke, pointing at the empty plastic container.

"That's it!" says John. Good, the ice is broken.

"Got a Phillips-head screwdriver?" he asks.

I'm not sure this is a joke.

"No. Maybe you can whittle one from a cut-down tree."

John laughs. Actually, he probably could do this, if he wanted to take the time.

"Well, give me those pliers. I can probably get the intake tube loose with them."

I dig the pliers out of my lunch bag. We still have a pair of snipper pliers and three plastic ties in reserve.

John disconnects the intake, and pours a small capful of gas into the carburetor opening. Then he gets back into the Jeep, leaving the hood up. When he cranks the starter, the engine still refuses to start. Without waiting for John to suggest it, I reach down and put my hand over the intake tube, feeling a solid rush of suction. Then I pull it away quickly, and the engine almost starts. I've seen John do this on finicky engines before.

"That was me!" I yell to John, out of sight on the other side of the hood.

I put my hand back over the intake, and yell: "Try again!"

The engine coughs again when I use my hand to battle the suction, but it doesn't start. John stops cranking, and comes back around front to join me in front of the engine.

"You did that?" he asks.

"I just put my hand over that tube," I say, pointing to the intake. "Seemed like it almost started."

"You were acting like a choke," he notes. "So it looks like the problem is fuel, after all."

"Try cranking it, while I act like the choke," says John.

I climb aboard, and rotate the key. In just a few seconds, the engine starts and continues to run smoothly.

"That did it!" says John.

I'm immensely proud of my accomplishment. Wayne-the-Choke is the hero of the moment. But what does this mean about the next time we try to start this engine in the middle of nowhere. Without a toolbox.

In a few minutes, we're underway. Bro is in the back, while I get to ride in a real seat. However, there's no door; only a rubber-coated wire clipped across the side of the vehicle. It would prevent nothing from falling out of the Jeep, including me. But I latch it anyway.

"I locked the door," I announce.

John laughs as I snap the wire into place.

I glance at the three red lights on the speedometer in front of John labeled "Brake," "Seatbelts," and "Battery." They're basically meaningless, since there are no seatbelts, and although the parking brake does stick until John wiggles the lever, the light simply stays illuminated. I'm interested in the "Battery" light, but it goes out as I'm watching it.

As we pull onto the main logging road, there's a fairly steep uphill turn, and John stalls the Jeep.

"It was running rough just before it stalled," says John. "Probably won't restart."

It does, but only after several tries.

"What about the alternator," I ask. "Could it have anything to do with any of this if the battery isn't charging properly?"

I remember the "Battery" light, so it makes sense to me that it's worth consideration. John shrugs it off immediately.

"Not related," he proclaims, but I know the thought has slid into the back of his mind for further action, if needed.

We stop at the first narrow spot in the logging road where alders are protruding from the edges and mini-trees grow in the center hump. We drove through this area yesterday without stopping, but now we're cleaning things up more thoroughly. John stops and shuts down the engine, ready to prune for a while.

I'm worried when he chooses to shut the engine down rather than leave it running as we cut the brush. But I know John is concerned about wasting gas. It's always this way. When I pull up next to him on my quad to talk briefly during a ride, he always tells me to turn off my engine. When we use a generator to run power tools, it's my job to turn it off between tasks, and then restart the generator a few minutes later when it's needed again. I've watched him use a drill to install a screw, and then ask me to turn the generator off while he changes to a larger drill bit. Saving gas is an enviable goal. John sometimes carries it to extremes.

"I'll get the little trees in the center of the road," I suggest.

"Leave them. We can just ride over them. It's the branches at the sides that are the problem. They whack you when you ride by."

This is true in the Jeep. But the center-of-road obstacles are more ominous for a quad, and they'll grow to become a real hazard. The alders on the sides do whack through the non-doors of the Jeep, but a quad travels a narrower path, and I always ride with a helmet. So it seems to me the centerline mini-trees are worth some attention.

John wins, of course, but I snip a few of the middle-of-road trunks when he isn't looking. Once he catches me: "Forget those. Cut the sides," he chides.

When we try to restart the Jeep, it struggles again. This time we need to pop the hood, and huddle over the small engine while John wiggles some more wires. I notice he reaches down and shakes an ugly, loose-looking connection next to the alternator. It's only a token, but I appreciate it.

When John tries starting the engine again, it jumps to life. So it seems something he touched did the trick. What it was is a complete mystery. Of course, I imagine it's the alternator.

We drive a little farther, and come to a stop at the next spot that needs pruning.

"Maybe we should leave it running," says John.

I'm surprised but pleased. Then John ponders the situation for a moment, and shuts the engine down.

After cutting alders along the sides of this stretch of the dirt road (where I secretly snip another center obstacle), we get back in the Jeep. The engine cranks without any indication of firing. Then, after waiting a few minutes and trying again, the motor finally starts, runs rough, and then smooths to its normal sewing machine hum.

"Maybe we shouldn't shut it off again," concedes John.

I hope he's serious this time, since our distance from the Hole is increasing.

We continue to the Chippewa Bay logging dock, where we plan to stop (engine running, I hope) for lunch. When we pull into the parking area, John asks me: "Do you want to go down to the dock?"

"Sure, but let's leave it running."

"We'll be down there for a while."

"Just a few minutes," I challenge.

Without further consultation, John reaches for the key, and turns it off.

"It's not a problem if it doesn't start," he states.

"Why?" I ask. "We're a long way from home."

"But here's what we could do," says John. "We could walk back to your cabin, and get the raft. Then we could tow the raft to this dock to get the Jeep."

Sure, if you don't mind walking for about four hours, then towing a raft for another two hours, loading the Jeep, and motoring slowing back to Hole in the Wall. Of course, John loves challenges like this.

"But where would we off-load the Jeep once we get back to the Hole?" I counter.

"We could tow it to the Shinglemill tomorrow, and then put it on a trailer and drive it back to my house. That would be almost quicker than driving out through Theodosia."

It's another all-day project that I must admit sounds interesting. Heck, I'd do it!

"Are you still planning to take the Jeep back to town today?" I ask, realizing the daylight is now getting short.

"There's still time," replies John. "But I don't know about this engine going all that way. Probably should work on it some more here before I leave.

"And we can get some more tools from my cabin, if we need them," I add.

"Tools? Don't need many tools."

It's a good thing, because at present, we only have two pairs of pliers and the plastic ties, and a raft back at my cabin.

* * * * *

After lunch on the logging dock, the engine starts a lot better than expected. We don't even need to pop the hood, but the engine struggles enough to remind us all isn't well.

John wants to try climbing up towards Heather Main, just to see the condition of the road. Coming down two days ago was easy. Going up may be a bit of a challenge. Of course, this will take us even farther from home, and a steep road is a good place to stall a Jeep. But I must admit I'm now almost as much into this defy-the-odds adventure as John. Besides, we theorize we can always do a pop-the-clutch rolling start as long as we're on a hill. We should be able to turn the Jeep around on a hill and get a good roll headed downhill in neutral.

As we begin the climb towards Heather Main, we spook a grouse from the side of the road. The big bird, rather than hopping off into the brush at the side of the trail, runs ahead of us. It's strange behavior, but maybe related to an attempt to divert us from its new hatch. Mamma's new brood is probably nearby, and this will redirect our attention. The bird, a Blue Grouse (also called a Sooty Grouse) sports bright-orange combs above its eyes. It flounders in its half-flying, mostly stumbling mode, for several hundred metres, fluttering only inches above the ground in short semi-circular arcs, landing every few metres. Then, with its dark tail fanned out, the Blue Grouse struts a short distance before flapping its wings rapidly against the ground. Rather than fly, it whacks its wings against the ground. If it weren't for the hum of the Jeep's engine, we'd hear its territorial *thump-thump-thump*. This is the same sound Margy and I often hear in the distance during quiet days at Hole in the Wall.

The grouse finally jumps out of sight into the thick bushes at the edge of the road. It seems like a distinct game the bird is playing with us, but it's more likely an important strategy to protect its fledglings.

We climb towards Heather Main in low gear, but then John announces that he detects a miss in the engine, something I can't hear. To me, the engine is continuing to hum along, but I don't trust this motor. If we shut it off or John stalls on a steep grade, we might be stuck.

Sure enough, the engine runs noticeably rougher, even to me. After lugging down in low gear, on a fairly steep grade, the Jeep's motor stops.

John cranks and cranks to no avail. Even wiggling the wires under the hood leads to nothing. We're finally stranded.

Or are we. This is the hill we'd hoped for, if we were to lose the engine. Except, we'll need to turn the Jeep around first, more easily said than done.

The Jeep is much heavier than I'd estimated. And even with John's noteworthy strength and my puny (by comparison) contribution, we can barely move the vehicle. We do manage to get it partially turned around, but the road isn't wide enough to complete the maneuver. Once angled downhill, the Jeep's wide turning radius causes us to come to the edge of the road (and a sharp drop-off) before completing the turn. We place a rock under the front tire as a chock, while John contemplates the situation. We don't have enough strength to overcome the force of gravity that's now ready to pull the Jeep downhill. Trying to push it back uphill is well beyond our strength.

"We'll cut down a tree and make a big pry bar," says John.

So I was wrong. He wouldn't whittle a screwdriver out of a tree, but he might construct a pry bar.

Using my chainsaw, John selects an already-dead alder along the side of the road with a trunk diameter of about eight inches. Once he cuts it, he trims off the branches, and we haul the 10-foot log to the front of the Jeep. Using a big rock for leverage, we both push on the pry bar, while John uses his (momentarily) spare hand to move the rock used as a safety chock with each small movement of the Jeep. In tiny spurts, we manage to move the Jeep about a half metre, reinserting the chock as we go. It's just enough for John to carefully complete the turn to an adequate downhill angle.

John positions himself in the Jeep for the pop-the-clutch start, while I question to myself how this is going to work. How we'll get the chock out isn't clear, but together we somehow manage it. One of John's hands dangles outside the Jeep, precariously pulling back uphill on the pry bar, keeping the pressure off the rock, while I quickly kick it free. We're rolling!

Children, get all of your hands and feet out of the way! I run behind the Jeep, and give it a solid push downhill. John pops the clutch, the engine catches, and then runs smoothly.

It's enough to persuade even John to make sure this is our last stop on the way home.

* * * * *

When we finally pull into our makeshift parking spot next to the quads, John wants to let the Jeep sit awhile, and then try a cold start.

"We haven't tried a really cold start since we left today," says John.

"How about vapor lock?" I ask. "I know this isn't a fuel-injected engine, but can't you still have vapor lock?"

"Not likely," he replies. "I think its ignition rather than fuel. Do you have a plug wrench?"

"No, just the two pairs of pliers and the plastic ties."

Once again, I'm sure John has stored away my comments regarding vapor lock, and will mull it over later. But he's not about to give in to me by indicating my theory might have credence.

We wait another ten minutes, and then he cranks the starter again. While I stand in front of the open hood watching the lose wires and the transparent fuel filter that leads to the carburetor, I notice the filter is almost full with clean-looking gas, with a wide air gap at the top. When the starter rotates the engine, the fuel filter fills immediately with fuel, but then I see bubbles flowing in the filter, small but easily seen. As the engine cranks, they continue to flow, and then disappear when the engine finally starts to fire. The motor catches and continues to run.

"Come look at this!" I say to John.

John leaves the motor running and comes around to the front of the Jeep.

"The fuel filter had small bubbles inside as your were cranking. Now it's clear again."

"No way," replies John.

I reach over to the filter, figuring there's no danger touching it with the engine running. When I push against it, a sudden surge of big bubbles pass through the filter.

"Man, it's vapor lock!" exclaims John. "Look at those bubbles!"

Now he reaches for the filter himself, pushes it, and more bubbles tumble downstream.

"It's leaking," says John. "It's dripping right at the bottom, pulling air inside and cutting off the flow of fuel. We've found it!"

Maybe yes. Maybe no. Who knows what he'll find tomorrow. In fact, a few days later, when John works on the Jeep more thoroughly at home, he determines the ignition coil is defective, replaces it, and the Jeep runs flawlessly for many more months. Then, of course, it stops running for some other reason.

But for today, "we" have found at least part of an elusive problem, and conquered an engine that's determined to strand us. Tools or no tools.

Chapter 9

Lake Dreams
Chippewa Bay, Powell Lake

"Foguary" deals its regular hand. For two weeks in mid-January, the fog comes and goes on a regular basis, making plans on the lake subject-to-change. The second month of Foguary (February) will probably follow suit, but we settle into the flow.

When the sun occasionally pokes above the trees at sunrise (9:30 am across the bay behind John's Cabin Number 2), Margy and I rejoice. Of course, the "ball of fire" is more of a muted yellow orb, glowing meekly through the low stratus. But it's the sun, and reason to celebrate. After solarless days for weeks on end, just to know where Sol is located in the sky seems a modest victory.

We decide to chase the sun to Chippewa Bay, where it'll stay above the trees longer than the three brief hours allotted to Hole in the Wall this time of year. At our cabin, with a forested shoreline on the cliff to the south, winter days are short. In Chippewa Bay, even with the massive Bunster Range to the west, we'll have another hour of afternoon sunshine. That is, if the orb stays visible through the two layers of clouds – low stratus and high cirrus.

Any excuse for a boat ride is a happy event, especially with our skookum new Hewescraft hardtop. Purchased five months ago, the 200-horsepower outboard has logged only 40 hours so far, and we look for any reason to go for on boat trip. The kicker has even fewer hours, not even enough to reach its break-in oil change at 10 hours.

So we start off today using the 9.9-horsepower Yamaha kicker. It pushes us slowly southward through First Narrows, past Sandy Beach, and out into the open area of the lower lake we call the North Sea.

The water is quiet – not a single boat in sight – all the way down to the south end of the lake near the Shinglemill. No logging crew boats; no runabouts plying their way to their cabins; no signs of activity anywhere, except our Hewescraft chugging slowly along.

Margy drives, navigating around the headlands into Chippewa Bay, and then north towards the logging dock that's soon to drop into the muted shadows of the Bunsters. Today we cruise slowly, taking the long way to the dock, circling the entire bay along the way. On our right, the few float cabins occupying this notoriously rough bay slide past. Here, winds called CB-CB'ers originate – Chippewa Bay Cabin Busters. But today the water is as calm as it ever gets.

Past the last cabin, Margy turns left to parallel the north shore at the head of the bay. This is one of the warmest and sandiest beaches on the lake. The water here is also the focal point for big waves.

We travel past "The Point," where we've explored for relics of the past when the lake is at its lowest water level. The Point is the site of some old logging camp cabins, flooded when the dam at the paper mill was constructed a hundred years ago.

Next is the wide jungle of snags poking high out of the water, sporting dozens of birdhouses fabricated by logging crews of recent vintage, and an osprey nest now vacant for the winter season. The logging ramp and dock are next, protected from the storms by a double-line of boom logs.

Approaching the dock, I go back to the swim grid, throttling the small Yamaha to idle, and shifting out of gear. Then I yell to Margy: "Start the main engine, but keep it in neutral until I've secured the kicker."

Once the big engine is operating, I shutdown the kicker and remove the steering bar connecting it to the bigger outboard.

"Okay, you can take us in now," I holler forward. "The fenders are set up for the left side."

Margy slowly maneuvers inside the breakwater boom, and sets up for a nice approach to a port-side docking. But the wind is from the south, holding us away from the dock. So the boat ends up perfectly positioned parallel to the dock, but six feet from the railing, and slowly drifting farther away. Margy backs away, and tries again. This time, she pushes up against the dock in perfect form. I hop off and secure the lines.

When the engine is turned off, we stand next to the boat on the dock, pausing to absorb our surroundings. The sun is barely visible through the clouds, within minutes of setting behind the Bunsters at 1 o'clock in the afternoon.

The lake remains calm and quiet, with one boat now in sight far to the south, headed down the lake towards the Shinglemill. The only noise is the distant *whop-whop* of the Coast Guard helicopter that routinely practices search and rescue operations in the lower section of the lake. The chopper is out of sight, but the big military-size rotors churn out tremendous energy at an RPM that seems too slow to support such a big machine. Hovering a few metres above the water, rescue divers are probably being lowered on strong cables that take them down to surface of the lake. They'll do this for hours at a time, but today it's a distant sound, occasionally changing in pitch as the load on the personnel cables causes slight adjustments in the chopper's power settings. I picture the big helicopter, perched motionless a few metres above the lake, hovering low and blasting concentric circles of waves outward.

"Maybe John's up there, keeping an eye on us," I say to Margy, motioning to the top of the Bunsters south of the dock.

"Wouldn't be surprised," she replies. "He'll probably phone tonight and tell us he saw me trying to dock, and wondered why it took two tries."

A few weeks ago, while gathering firewood on Sandy Beach in our small tin boat, John watched us from his favourite Powell Lake lookout in the Bunsters. It's a spot not easily accessed by quad, requiring a lengthy ride form Southview Road or the alternate route from Sliammon Lake.

"Hey, I saw you at Sandy Beach today," he said when he phoned that evening. "At first, all I could see was a tiny red dot, which was your tin boat. But I figured it was you, and after awhile I could make out two people on the beach."

John's vision is amazingly acute, and he sees things no one else can perceive. In addition to his perfect eyesight, he seems to be everywhere. "I saw you today," he'll say quite often. Maybe it was when I was in back of City Motors getting propane containers filled, or in the North Harbour, cleaning my boat at the dock. John is literally everywhere, and he misses nothing. I wouldn't be surprised to find he's looking down on us right now from his perch in the Bunsters.

Margy and I cross over the bridge to shore, and walk the logging road up to the main creek, where water tumbles down from the mountains above. We stand watching the flow come out from under the bridge, as it drops precipitously into the steep ravine and Powell Lake, out of sight below.

When we return to our boat, there's still no activity visible on the lake, even to the distant south. The sky is covered by a thin, high overcast, and the sun has set behind the mountains, but the visibility in all directions is outstanding.

We're planning a trip to Hawaii next week, a jaunt to find a few days of sunshine, something I find helpful in the heart of winter. By comparison, many would consider Powell Lake to be gloomy.

Hewescraft at Chippewa Dock

"When we get to Maui, I'm going to remind you of this," I say to Margy. "While we're basking in the sun, I might ask if you want to stay in Hawaii forever."

"And I'll reply that I'll take Powell Lake any day," Margy replies. "Sun or no sun."

She's right. This place is magic, and we know it, and we both thrive on the magnitude of its earthy power.

* * * * *

Leaving the logging dock, I'm in the driver's seat. I maneuver outside the boom logs, turn south along the shore, and quickly bring the boat up on plane. As soon as we're stable, my cell phone rings. I come back all the way on the throttle, and shift into neutral.

Taking my phone from my pocket, I flip it open, noticing the text accompanying the incoming call: "Caller Unknown," so I don't expect it to be anybody I know.

"Hello, this is Wayne," I say, while hearing the scratch of static in the background.

A voice I don't recognize says something, and then the line seems dead.

"I'm in a weak coverage area," I say. "Can you hear me at all?"

"Wayne. Hey, this is Rick. Can you hear me?"

"Rick! Oh, hi."

"Hey, where are you? Is that you just pulling out from the Chippewa Bay dock?"

I laugh, knowing where he must be to see me here. "I should have known!" I reply. "You're up in the Bunsters."

"Hold on a minute," says Rick. "I'll let you talk to John."

As John comes to the phone, Margy has figured out what's going on, and she's laughing. John's voice is typically enthusiastic.

"Hey, I asked Mike to hand me the binoculars. I told him it looks like freakin' Wayne down there in his boat!"

"That's us," I say. "Margy's grinning from ear to ear. We figured you might be watching us. Is that freakin' you, up there watching freakin' us?"

"You betcha!" laughs John.

So here we are, one of the few boats on huge Powell Lake in February, motoring out of remote Chippewa Bay. And being looked down upon by an ever-present John.

Things won't be like this in Hawaii.

* * * * *

AFTER MOVING OUR QUADS TO HOLE IN THE WALL, they don't go back to town at the end of summer. Having our ATVs near our cabin is convenient, and a quicker process for riding than going to town. Margy and I can ride from Hole in the Wall on short notice, and spend less time getting to and from our bikes. The disadvantage is that our routes are limited. Every trip starts with the trail to Chippewa Bay, since it is the only way out of the Hole. From there, it's either Museum Main or up the mountain to Heather Main. Although Theodosia Valley and Olsen's Main are available to us from Heather Main, it's an all-day trip back and forth. So we're constantly on the lookout for another means to increase the variety of our trips, while keeping our preparation time at a minimum.

An obvious solution is a landing craft to quickly transport our quads anywhere on Powell and Goat Lake. If we can find an appropriate landing craft, the possibilities seem endless. Easier said than done.

I begin the search, assuming there are plenty of landing craft waiting for me in this hot boat buyer's market. Selling a boat had become difficult in recent years, but buyers find reasonable prices and plenty of excellent boats for sale. Except for landing craft, where availability is minimal.

I watch the Internet sales sites for coastal British Columbia, even the entire province of BC and the state of Washington. Most available landing craft are too big for efficiency (with an accompanying high price tag) or too small to handle two quads. When the occasional just-right landing craft appears on the market, it's way too expensive, yet sells quickly.

One model that occasionally appears in advertisements is the Sea Truck, a classic design that's a bit oversized for our needs, but gets my attention. A common problem with most moderate-sized (less than 28-foot) landing craft is their cab size and placement. Their enclosed space is often too large and too far forward, wasting the 14 feet of deck space we need for our two quads.. The Sea Truck has a far-aft cab, and its enclosed area is modular in construction, so the ramp space can be increased or decreased to meet the user's need.

I find a 26-foot Sea Truck on the Internet that's supposedly available in Nanaimo, but I phone to find it's already sold. Similarly, a Sea Truck in Gibsons appears on Craigslist. I telephone the next day while I'm passing through the area on Highway 101, headed for the Vancouver ferry. The seller takes my name and phone number, just in case a pending deal with someone from Harrison Lake falls through. The buyer is expected to arrive in Gibsons on the incoming northbound ferry, the same ship I'll be taking south in a few hours. I never hear from the seller again.

Trapper Jim, moored near my Hewescraft at the Shinglemill, has a beautiful 24-foot landing craft, although there's only 12-feet of useable loading length. This means one quad needs to ride awkwardly on the ramp, a difficult arrangement for Margy and me. Jim isn't interested in selling his boat, but it's a good example of how challenging it'll be to find a moderate-sized landing craft that meets our needs.

Then I find Fred. He lives on Hardy Island during the warm months, travelling to Hawaii during the winter. He's planning to sell (soon) his 24-foot self-propelled barge. Technically, it's not a landing craft, since it has a flat, enclosed top deck. Without a hinged front-ramp, usable deck space extends right up to the bow. It meets our specs for a 14-foot loading length (plus an additional 5 feet), and includes skookum portable metal ramps for getting our quads to shore. This barge won't set any speed records with its small 50-horsepower outboard, but the vessel looks really good, and the price is right.

One limitation is the timing of the sale. It'll be several months before Fred will be back from Hawaii, and then he'll need to use the barge for a few weeks to resupply his Hardly Island cabin in preparation for summer. The vessel is currently stored on shore at his cabin on a hefty marine way that he built. His plan is to launch in mid-April, during a spring tide near full moon. This is the first time he's used a marine way during the winter – in former years the barge was pulled out of the water at nearby Hummingbird Cove, using a marina sling. This year, he'll use his tractor to ease the boat off the marine way at high tide.

Barge on Fred's marine way

We plan to meet at Saltery Bay a few days after the barge's April launch, where I'll be able to inspect the vessel and ride with Fred on a sea trial. However, I'm already convinced this boat is for me, so there'll be no backing out on this deal. In fact, my biggest concern is losing the sale to someone else, although Fred has given me reassuring words that I'll maintain first-buy opportunity for the vessel. Still, I feel better when I mail Fred a hefty deposit (my choice), and notice my online banking account shows the cheque has been cashed a few days later. Sight unseen (and we all know about the reliability and currency of photos on Craigslist), I've bought the barge.

Early on the morning before our planned meeting at Saltery Bay, my phone rings. Fred sounds a bit distressed.

"Wayne, I'm afraid the launch didn't go as planned."

My imagination races to an image of the barge smashed against the rocks.

"Nothing serious," he adds. "Just couldn't get it into the water during yesterday's high tide."

"Oh, no problem," I reply, happy to dispense with thoughts of losing the barge before I even see it in person.

"The tide wasn't high enough," says Fred. "I looked things over, and didn't want to push it down the ramp. I've got to go back to Nanaimo this week, so I'll look over the tide tables, and come back for another try in May. In the meantime, I'll consult with a friend who knows more about these things than I do."

It sounds like he has his own version of John to assist him, so I understand. But launching in May implies he wants to wait for the next full moon, which means another full month. I'm anxious to get the barge, although I'm sure Fred knows more about the limitations of his marine way than I do. Still, I offer some assistance.

"Can I come over there and help?" I ask. "I could bring as many bodies with me as you think are needed."

"It's not a matter of needing more muscle," replies Fred. "The tractor is plenty. I'm just worried about hurting the barge if the tide isn't high enough."

In just a few seconds, my brain goes through several scripts before I reply. Could we use my boat to pull the stern of the barge towards the water? How about jacking up the boat, and greasing the metal stringers on the bottom of the barge and the wooden tracks of the marine way? Fortunately, I immediately realize Fred knows more about marine ways and boats than I'll never know. So I say nothing except: "I understand, Fred. Thanks for letting me know."

"You bet," replies Fred, sounding relieved I'm not complaining about the unexpected delay. "I'll bring two truckloads of cabin supplies back with me on my next trip from Nanaimo, so we can minimize how long I need the barge once it's floating again. I'll keep you posted."

I know he will. And for that I'm grateful. The barge should still be ready for the beginning of summer, but my biggest concern is the additional time might provide more opportunities for the deal to fall through. Although Fred sounds completely sincere, I travel down the lake the next day, send a second totally unsolicited deposit to him in Nanaimo, and anxiously wait to see it clear in my bank account.

* * * * *

With May just begun, and the approaching spring tide still two weeks away, Margy and I ride our quads up Museum Main from Chippewa

Bay, in an attempt to visit the nicely preserved steam donkey that lies at the top. The spring bushes are now nearly fully grown along the road, hopefully enough to blot out the view down to Powell Lake at the critical section that previously stopped Margy in her tracks (literally). It's a unique fear of heights that manifests itself when there's a sheer drop-off to the side during a steep climb or descent. Today, unfortunately, the bushes haven't grown enough, and Margy grinds to a halt.

"Don't push it, if you don't feel good about it," I suggest.

I've learned over time that once her drop-off fear sets in, it won't suddenly get better. Margy is a licenced pilot, and a good one, but I've known many pilots (me included, at least a little) who have a fear of heights. For me, looking over the side of a bridge or a tall building can do it. There's just something in an airplane regarding not being connected to the ground that makes everything okay, regardless of height.

"Maybe I can hike up the hill for a little while, if you'll drive my quad up," says Margy, in a valiant mood.

"Sure," I reply. "But we really don't need to do this."

"I'll give it a try," she replies.

So I drive her quad up to the turnout, where the main swerves sharply to the right. From there, the drop-off is still steep, but there's no view of the lake below. Maybe it'll make a difference.

Margy trudges on foot to catch up with me, glances up the road to the right, and looks scared.

"I don't think I can do it," she says reluctantly.

"No problem. Let's head back down."

So down we go, me driving Margy's quad slowly, using the engine in low gear as a brake, while she walks along side (on the uphill edge of the road away from the sloping escarpment). When we arrive back at my quad, I transfer to it, and Margy climbs aboard her bike. Slowly (because the terror she's fighting isn't over), I follow her back down Museum Main. At the bottom, we turn right, and ride to the Chippewa Bay logging dock.

We park our bikes near the bridge to the dock, and walk down to the big float where no boats are tied up today. Huge logging booms spread in all directions, empty for now. This is where we'll arrive with our new barge someday soon, preparing to on-load our quads for the

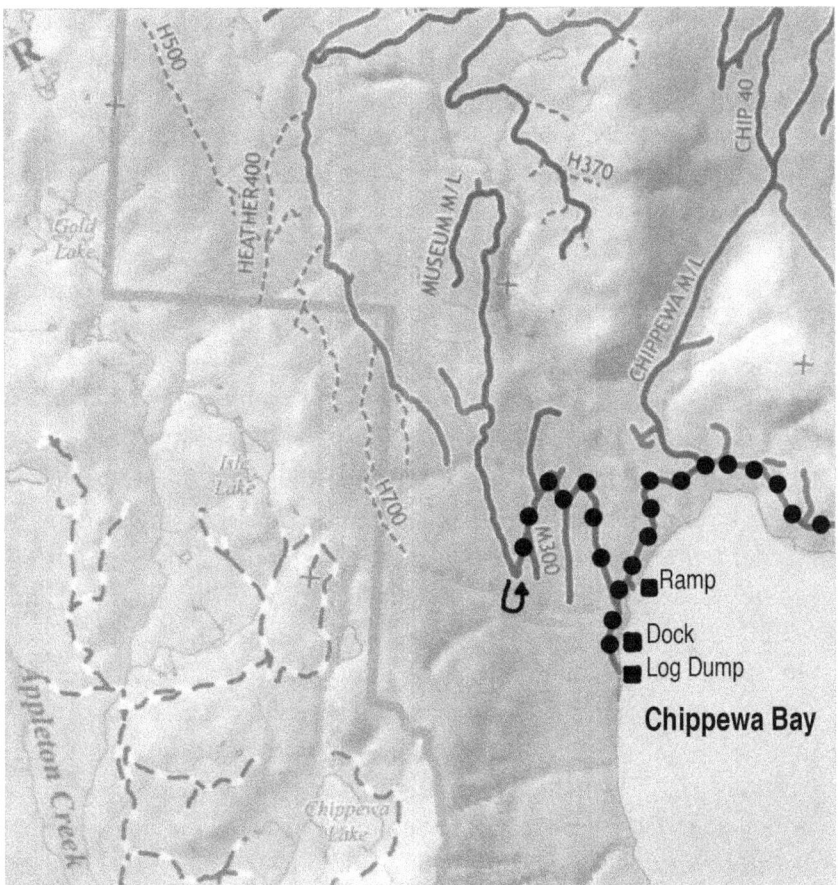

first time at the barge ramp a little farther up the shore. Today's visit to Chippewa Bay is a preview of that much-anticipated event, our minds racing ahead to the historic (to us) day when we'll begin our exploration of the numerous logging roads that originate at the many barge ramps on Powell Lake.

As we stand on the dock, I ponder an idea.

"You know, that bridge down to he dock is just wide enough for a quad," I comment, anticipating Margy's reply.

"You're not really considering that, are you?"

"No, just a thought, because it would work. That's what John and I did with our raft at the head of the lake. We were going to use the barge ramp, but it was easier just to tie up to the dock and off-load our quads over the bridge to shore."

"Kinda' chancy," Margy remarks.

She's right. Doing something like that without John wouldn't be wise. The water here is a lot deeper than the height of a quad, in case something goes wrong.

"I know," I reply. "But it would work. I was just thinking about how far apart this dock is from the barge ramp. Usually they're right next to each other, but not here. Still, it'll be an easy on-load at the barge ramp."

Margy looks relieved that another dumb idea has died a quick death.

After leaving the dock, we ride up the road to check out the barge ramp. I'm surprised to find the water shallower than expected. It's a beach of small rocks, with foot-deep water extending out a few metres, and then an adequate drop-off. Maybe it'll look more appealing when the lake level rises, which is what's happening now as spring progresses. I wonder if the barge will ground itself before reaching shore, requiring us to put our loading ramps in the shallow water rather than on solid ground. Quads travel fairly well in shallow water. They're not called "all-terrain vehicles" for nothing. Just don't try driving in too deep or your low-pressure tires will cause your quad to float, which isn't a good thing.

While Margy watches, I drive into the shallow water, and turn around so I'm facing shore. I'm trying to duplicate my quad's position as it will go onto the barge, but then I realize I'm completely backwards, since we'll be driving straight onto the barge.

So I ask myself why I'm facing this way. But since I'm here now, I might as well experiment by shifting into reverse and back out a ways to test the traction in water like I might experience near the barge. However, I'm temporarily jammed on the rocks, so I add a little throttle. A little too much.

My quad breaks loose from its temporarily stuck position, leaps over the rock that's acting as a chock, and suddenly I'm floating. The water pours over my running boards, and my feet are getting soaked, as water seeps into my boots. Quickly, I reach down to shift out of reverse, hoping the forward spin of my wheels in the water will propel me back to a solid surface. Of course, my quad does what all quads do when you attempt to shift in a hurry – the lever jams. I fiddle with the shifter, finally changing gears, and throttle up to an unusual sensation of nothing happening as the wheels spin. My bike begins to gyrate sideways and slowly forward, using its tires as paddle wheels. Then I feel the firm grip of the rocks. Without further delay, I quickly drive out of the water.

Meanwhile, Margy has been watching from shore, without a lot of concern. She knows I'm only in a foot of water, and maybe she didn't even recognize I was floating. It's just Wayne doing something stupid for no apparent reason.

"A little too deep," I say, as I pull up beside her quad. "I was floating."

"Oh," she replies. "Probably shouldn't do something like that when it's time to load our quads on the barge."

She's right. I probably shouldn't.

Chapter 10

Lake Barge
Saltery Bay and Powell Lake

FRED SUCCESSFULLY LAUNCHES THE BARGE at high tide, and we arrange a sea trial and a date to transfer the boat. Of course, the complicated simple life requires a plan that's as convoluted as possible. The trip to Hardy Island for the sea trial is no exception.

Although Fred offers to bring the barge to Saltery Bay, I suggest meeting him at his cabin on Hardy Island. It will be a good opportunity for an overnight trip in my Bayliner 2452, so I plan to visit Fred's place first, and then motor over to Ballet Bay on nearby Nelson Island for an evening on anchor. However, we don't want to leave John out of this special event, so we arrange to stop at Saltery Bay first to pick him up. To make sure things are adequately complicated, Margy and I will be returning from the States that afternoon on Pacific Coastal Airlines from Vancouver. We'll then rush down to Westview's North Harbour, launch the Bayliner for Saltery Bay to meet John and Bro, and then motor over to Hardy Island for the sea trial. After this, we plan to return John and Bro to Saltery Bay, and then proceed to Ballet Bay for our overnight anchorage, followed by our return to Powell River the next morning. It'll be a boat trip of less than 24 hours with a track squiggling back-and-forth across our GPS moving map.

It all works flawlessly (except for a "bad seas" return to Powell River the next morning). Our airliner lands at Powell River at 1:15 pm, and we pull past the ferry dock at Saltery Bay at 3:15, tying up briefly at the government dock to load John and Bro. This time of year

Saltery Bay

(May) the dock sports lots of open moorage, so I park near the end of the main finger.

It's a quick trip across to Hardy Island, and Fred is waiting for us when we arrive. We tie up at his dock, where the barge is parked. Since first seeing the advertisement for the barge on Craigslist, I've been infatuated with this vessel. Finally, I'm going riding on the barge!

It's an easy sea trial, since I'm already totally sold. First, Fred briefs me on the barge's mechanical systems. It's a simple vessel that's built skookum-strong and maintained to perfection.

"Only one thing you need," says John, as Fred pulls off the outboard motor's cover for a closer look.

"I suppose I need a bigger engine," I say, knowing how much John would like a faster barge to carry us quicker to our quad-riding destinations.

"How'd you guess?" quips John.

"Sure, we'll get one," I say. "But not until this engine dies."

The 50-horsepower motor is probably going to outlive us all. And it meets all of my needs for Powell Lake. I'm sure of it. Still, I pretend I'm listening to John's plea for a 110-horse Yamaha.

Arrival at Hardy Island

"You're gonna' want to go faster," says John. "You always do."

"But that's on the chuck. You know I'm always anxious to get home to my cabin. Heck, I'll be willing to go plenty slow on Powell Lake, maybe trolling for trout along the way."

Inspecting the barge

Engine inspection

John is right – I'm not usually enthused about going slow on the water. But this time will be different.

"Good engine," says Fred. "Nearly bulletproof."

Just what John didn't want to hear.

In the cab, Fred talks me through the barge's other basic systems. Then it's time for the sea trial. I feel like I've already lived this in my mind, and there are no surprises. We motor around for a few minutes at 3600 RPM, and then Fred adds full power to demonstrate the maximum speed characteristics. Since the cab is small, John, Margy, and Bro are on the outside deck. Bro explores the bow, while Margy and John sit on the deck with their backs against the front of the cab. I can imagine John saying to Margy: "So that's the top speed, I guess." When he gets on a bandwagon, he never gets off.

I'm very happy with this boat, and I know John is, too. Although I'll be the new owner, John will have full access to the barge. It's a perfect arrangement for both of us. We'll get lots of use out of this vessel, mainly for recreation with our quads. But John will enjoy using it to bring building materials up the lake. In fact, he already has a pile of heavy-duty plywood sitting in his back yard, ready for the barge to arrive at Powell Lake.

Bro on bow

Fred invites us to walk the short distance to his cabin. He has created an amazingly comfortable home on Hardy Island. Everything is, of course, top quality, and his personal workmanship shows

Barge lovers unite

everywhere we go. Along the trail to the cabin, Fred proudly shows us his tractor. Then, sitting in the next bend of the trail is something that really gets John's attention – a mini-excavator resting on its deployed stabilizing legs.

"Wow, look at that, Wayne!" he says to me. "Could we ever use a machine like that for building trails!"

"Hey, we own a barge now," I reply. "And we know how to find this place. We'll just pop over when Fred's gone, and load 'er up."

Fortunately, Fred has a good sense of humour, and laughs it off. But if his excavator is suddenly missing, I know who Fred will call first.

Fred's cabin at Hardy Island

* * * * *

DELIVERY OF THE BARGE is scheduled for late May. I'll be back in the States then, so John prepares to accept the boat at Kent's Beach. He'll meet Fred and Jeff (who'll be bringing the big Valley Marine trailer) at the launch ramp near Saltery Bay. From there, the barge will be hauled to Jeff's shop, where it'll spend a few days getting ready for Powell Lake. The main project before launch at the Shinglemill involves the installation of a 9.9-horsepower kicker that'll be connected to the main fuel tank and electrical system (for electric start and tilt-trim, luxuries by my standards).

On the morning of the planned meeting at Kent's Beach, John phones me in Bellingham. The schedule is already falling apart.

"I talked to Jeff this morning," says John, sounding a bit upset. "He says the haul-out is tomorrow rather than today."

"Oops, I'm sure that's my fault. Our schedule has changed so many times, I probably got the date wrong when I talked to Jeff. I'll call him right now."

When I phone Jeff, he goes with the flow: "No worries," he says. "I can be there at 4 o'clock today."

So it all works out fine. Fred shows up with the barge, and turns it over to John and Jeff. After all of my anxious waiting for this day, it has finally arrived.

Barge on trailer at Saltery Bay

"Done!" announces John over the phone that evening. Which says it all. The barge is now sitting in Jeff's shop in Powell River.

To me, this feels like the beginning of a new era in my life. The barge will be a wonderful way to explore Powell Lake with our quads.

* * * * *

TWO DAYS LATER, JOHN AND JEFF LAUNCH THE BARGE at the Shinglemill, and John reports to me by phone that all goes well. John gets the honour of the first trip in the new (to us) vessel, hauling his plywood stash up the lake to his cabin.

"It worked out really good," says John. "Nice barge. Needs a bigger engine, of course."

Of course.

* * * * *

THE FOLLOWING SATURDAY, I arrive home in Powell River, and by late afternoon I'm in the cab of the barge that John has parked at the Shinglemill's public dock. I survey the simple instrument panel, ready to start the engine. But when I twist the key, nothing happens, not even a faint click of a starter relay closing. I check the position of the throttle, to make sure the neutral safety switch isn't preventing the engine from starting. The handle seems in the proper detent.

"Now where would you be if you were a battery switch?" I say to myself out loud.

It makes sense that John would have turned off the switch when he left the boat at the dock for me, but I don't find it clear sight. How about under the instrument panel? I bend down and look at the neatly bundled wires and the big red battery switch. I move it from *Off* to *Both*.

While Margy hovers in our Hewescraft near the dock, I successfully start the engine, and let it warm up while I start untying the dock lines. As I pull away from the Shinglemill, Margy snaps a photo of me proudly motoring out of the marina.

Margy heads up the lake in the speedy Hewescraft, while I plod along happily in the barge. I spend the next hour testing the vessel's performance. With the 50-horsepower outboard operating at a comfortable 3600 RPM, I cruise at 7 knots as verified by my portable GPS. It's a reasonable speed for me, although I admit to being a guy who normally insists on travelling on-plane. This will be, I'm sure, the

Barge at the Shinglemill

one exception to that normal demand. As I've tried to explain to John, I love this lake so much that it's the one place where slow is acceptable. Maybe barging along at 7 knots will wear off eventually, but I have this funny feeling the puny 50-horse will be my intimate friend for a very long time.

I switch over to the new 9.9-horsepower kicker. It drives the boat at a solid 4 knots, even at a low throttle setting (no demanding RPMs until the new motor is broken in). So the kicker speeds me along almost as fast as the main engine. I switch back to the 50-horse outboard, and practice the feel of things at various throttle settings up to 4000 RPM. There is little change in speed on my portable GPS.

My starts, stops, and test maneuvering add a little extra time to my first trip up the lake, but I still arrive at Hole in the Wall in an hour and a half. Finally, after months of dreaming about this barge, I'm home, parked at my cabin on Powell Lake.

Barge at Hole in the Wall

* * * * *

THE NEXT DAY, Margy and I are ready to load our quads for the first time. It's a typical complicated simple life itinerary. The first leg of the journey involves towing my tin boat behind the barge to Chippewa Bay. Things begin a bit sloppy, since I use the first-available towline for the tin boat, nothing more than a weak clothesline. *Snap!* – the line breaks twice even before I'm through First Narrows. The good news is the barge maneuvers easily as I turn around twice to recover the trailing boat. Finally, I switch to a stronger rope, and we're on our way.

As is typical of the route to Chippewa, the water's a bit rough, but the barge handles the challenge wonderfully, riding stable and comfortably in 3-foot waves.

At the Chippewa dock, we tie up the barge, and return to Hole in the Wall in the tin boat. It's a slow trip, with the big waves more exciting in the small boat than the hefty barge. I notice that Margy looks stressed by the conditions, as she rides in the front of the boat.

"You look like you're not having fun," I yell to her over the sound of the outboard motor and the slapping waves.

"Not so good," she says. "Big waves."

"I can slow down," I suggest.

"No, let's get this over with."

It's like running in the rain. We'll get soaked anyway, so let's get the trip over quickly.

Margy looks uncomfortable facing back towards me, seemingly frozen in place. But she probably doesn't want to look directly into the waves.

"Maybe you'd feel better if you swing around and face forward," I say.

"I'm okay," she says.

"Would you feel better if you were driving?" I ask.

"No way! Shut up and drive," she says, trying to act nonchalant.

Said by someone who would prefer to run in the rain.

As we approach Sandy Beach near First Narrows, I notice the good news.

"There's a bright line in the water," I yell forward to Margy.

We've become familiar with the appearance of lines in the water, both dark and bright. They represent changes in wind, and soon the waves are gone, with conditions smooth again.

When we arrive in the Hole, we tie up near our quads' parking spot, and trek the short distance to ready our bikes for the trip to Chippewa Bay. When I begin to remove the straps from the tarps covering our quads, I jump back: "Yikes!"

"What!" shouts Margy.

"Oh, nothing," I reply. "I thought it was a snake or something. Just water caught in the tarp. Made a hissing sound."

Snakes are not my favourite thing.

Margy finds a hornets nest wedged below the running board of her bike, inspects it closely, and then whacks it away with a stick.

"Inactive nest," she says. "I guess we haven't been here for a while."

When I open the back storage box on my quad, I jump in fright once again.

"Ants!"

It's not just a few small ants. My storage box is crawling with hundreds of huge black ants. They're crawling furiously all over my equipment, in and out of my gloves and noticeably concentrated in the vicinity of my helmet. There's no way I'm wearing those items today. I slam the lid of the box shut, and snap the latches closed. I'll ride without a helmet or gloves, no big deal for this short trip. But I'll cringe all the way to Chippewa, waiting for the ants to sneak out of the rear box and crawl all over me.

When I'm finally ready to crank up my quad, nothing happens. The dash indicator display is normal, but the starter doesn't react. I've been in this situation so many times I'm convinced it's operator error, but what is it this time?

"Won't start," I say to Margy.

Just when I'm convinced the battery is dead (or nearly so, since the dash display is still working), I finally recognize the problem.

"Should I put it in park?" I ask out loud.

"Might help," says Margy.

Normally, I store my quad with the shift lever in "park." Who knows what happened this time. But if a quad doesn't start, one of the first guesses should be you're in a gear other than park or neutral. *Vroom, vroom!* All is well again.

As we exit the rough trail that eventually leads to the easy-riding logging road, I realize there's an item I've forgotten. Bringing a chainsaw for this trip would have been wise. This trail hasn't been ridden in many weeks, and spring storms can take a toll. But we luck out today, and the way is clear.

Clear that is, except for the dense overgrowth of the trail in recent weeks. Spring brings a sudden spurt in nature's vegetation, and it doesn't take long for the bush to reclaim paths made by man. We bash our way through the encroaching plants.

As we drive towards Chippewa, a steady stream of bugs impact my sunglasses and whack against my mouth. Without my helmet and goggles, it's an uncomfortable ride. But this minor discomfort is overshadowed by the momentous nature of the occasion. Our quads are headed towards their new home aboard the barge.

When we arrive in Chippewa Bay, we park our quads at the barge ramp, and walk the logging road to the dock where our barge awaits. Then we motor back to the ramp, aiming shoreward.

I've thought this through often – how to approach the landing – but this is the first time for real. I slow to idle, timing my drift as best as I can. I turn off the motor and use the electric tilt-trim to raise the motor as we glide towards shore.

With practice, I'll learn it's almost always okay to keep the motor running right up to contact with the shore, since there's normally plenty of depth at the stern. Even then, a slight upward tilt (making sure the leg is deep enough for the pump to spurt its cooling water) is a good safety practice while operating in shallow depths.

Loading quads at Chippewa Bay

Good timing! The barge contacts the ramp with a mild (and not too exciting) crunch of gravel. We're aground, but we could have started our "beaching" preparations a bit earlier. For one thing, Margy and

I still have our boots on. Belatedly, we get out of our boots and into our water shoes so we can go to shore. We start our bikes, and allow them to warm up, and then manhandle the barge's metal ramps into position. Live and learn – a process to be improved by fits and starts over the next few weeks. It's a learning curve that builds gradually over time. But today we're fortunate – the wind has dissipated, and the barge stays obediently in position until we're ready to load.

The skookum metal ramps are perfect for the task – light enough for us to maneuver and long enough to provide a gradual upslope onto the barge. I drive the first quad aboard, then the second, pull the ramps onto the barge, and we're on our way! Our launch is nearly flawless, but I learn today that we need to have a clear plan as soon as the second ramp is retracted. Even in this light wind, the barge starts to swing, so we need to act fast (or, as we learn later, use a pike pole to keep the stern steady). Today, I push off from shore in a sloppy fashion, as the barge starts to swing, but all ends well.

On-load at Chippewa Bay

A little more than an hour later, back at Hole in the Wall, the barge sits at the dock, looking spiffy with the quads aboard. We'll spend the next day outfitting the cab with our camping gear, getting ready for some major adventures on Powell Lake.

Quads on barge at Hole in the Wall

Chapter 11

Goat

Goat Island, Powell Lake BC

One day when we're in town, we visit the Western Forest Products office. The reception desk is unoccupied, but a lanky figure that could be Mike is in one of the first offices along the wall.

Mike is a person we know. He briefs the Powell Lake Cabin Owners Association at our annual meetings, providing an overview of where logging activity can be expected on the lake in the next few seasons. Today I've come here hoping to find Mike, but the fellow in the office is someone else. Maybe it's a prerequisite of forestry management to be lanky and robust looking.

"Hi, I'm Wayne, and this is my wife, Margy," I say from the threshold of his door. "We live up the lake, and we're planning to use a barge we've just purchased to explore places from some of your dock locations."

"Hole in the Wall, isn't it?" he says. "Go by there all the time. I read one of your books."

"Oh, good, so you know about me. Let me show you the new boat."

I step inside his office, and place a black-and-white photocopy of a barge picture on his desk.

"Nice," he says. "Can haul a lot with that."

"Mostly just our quads. Which is why we bought it."

"Good. We've got lots of barge ramps where you can go ashore."

I explain that we want to know who to contact to get an idea of the current level of logging and road building activity near Western Forest Product ramps.

"I can help you with that," he says. "My name's Rudi. I'd suggest contacting Stuart or me, if you need updates on areas where we're working."

He holds out his hand, and I shake it. He shakes Margy's hand, too. In my few interactions with Western Forest Product employees, I've been impressed with their attitude. Some local quad riders say the forestry companies are determined to make off-road recreational riding difficult. From my experience, logging company employees are always helpful, and seem to encourage our travels.

Rudi quickly explains he's glad we're going to be using some of their ramps and roads. He's an obvious lover of the outdoors, and hands me two business cards, one for him and one for Stuart, who will be our contact after Rudi retires in two months.

Over the next few weeks, as Margy and I begin our exploration of Powell Lake backcountry, we keep in contact with Rudi and Stuart, always calling in advance to get the status of the ramps and roads we'll be using. Today Rudi gives us an overview of the barge ramps on the lake, providing names for locations that are sometimes different from what we've called them all these years.

As he points out barge ramps on a huge map of Powell Lake, I take notes. We leave Rudi's office armed with lots of information, including some great maps I'll cut up and organize in a 3-ring binder to carry in my quad.

* * * * *

A FEW DAYS LATER, ON JUNE 3, Margy and I motor out of Hole in the Wall in the barge for the first time. This will be an easy day-trip to a location I've always called "Clover Dock," since it's near Clover Lake. But Rudi has designated this as "Goat Island," which makes sense, since it's the primary logging dock on the island.

There's not much to pack, since we'll be returning before dark, and all of our quad riding equipment and most of our overnight camping gear are already stored aboard the barge. I've developed a short checklist of items that should go with us each time, such as my portable GPS. For years, we've explored new places with John as our guide, so there was no danger of getting lost. With the GPS tracking our path, even if we do get lost on our own, it'll be easy to retrace our path.

This time we're more prepared as we approach the barge ramp. We've donned our water shoes and gloves, and I've sent Margy out from the cab to start both of the quads, so they'll be already idling when we hit the shore. The tie-down straps have been removed, and I've moved the heavy loading ramps forward, ready to be pulled off the bow and dropped into position.

Approaching Goat Island Ramp

About 5 metres from shore, I shift into idle, turn off the engine, tilt the motor as high as it'll go, and glide the remaining distance. On future trips, I'll usually keep the motor running and tilted up slightly, which is the preferred method. This makes for a more efficient get-away, if needed during a balked landing. But today I'm not yet convinced of the accuracy of the depth-sounder and the draft of the outboard's leg. So we glide motorlessly to shore.

Off-loading is a piece of cake. It's amazing how quickly I've become comfortable with this barge and the process of beaching it. In fact, everything is so laid-back that I ask Margy if she'd like to drive her quad down the ramp (in reverse). She's confident with this vessel, too, as evidenced by her quick and relaxed answer: "Sure!"

Margy does a fine job aligning her wheels with the ramps and backing down onto the shore. Then I back my red quad off the barge, and park next to her silver one.

Goat Island off-load

"Hop aboard," I say to Margy. "Once I push us off shore, tilt the engine back down and get it started quickly."

"I'll be ready," she replies.

Once again, we're dealing with sloppy learn-as-you-go procedures that will improve with time. But it's all safe, and works out okay.

I send Margy back to the cab, while I drag the metal ramps aboard as quickly as possible. But similar to our first barge ramp departure at Chippewa Bay, the stern of the boat begins to drift as soon as the first big ramp is clear of the shore, and gets worse as the second ramp is disconnected. I counteract with a quick push on the bow, and a yell to Margy as I climb aboard.

"The ass is starting to drift, but the water's deep enough to get the engine going." I say. "Get the motor down, and start 'er up,"

I'm not sure Margy hears me from inside the cab, but she does a good job, starting the engine quickly, and counteracting the drift nicely as she backs out into deeper water.

We motor the short distance to the logging dock, where we tie up the barge, and then walk the short distance to our quads. Unlike Chippewa Bay, the logging dock and barge ramp are adjacent to each other here, making things easier and more efficient.

Once we're aboard our bikes, I'm underway first, climbing to the top of the logging staging area, and then turn around to drive back down to see what's delaying Margy. She removes her helmet and motions me over to her quad.

"I can't get rid of my lockers," she says when I pull up beside her.

"Why were you using your lockers?" I ask.

"I guess I hit the switch when I was backing up after we off-loaded our bikes. I don't remember doing it, but the red light is on. Now I can't get it to turn off."

"Let me give it a try," I suggest.

She steps off her bike, and I hop aboard. I hit the switch for the differential lockers, but the red light remains illuminated. Switching back and forth between four-wheel-drive and lockers doesn't change anything either.

"I'll take it up the hill," I say. "Maybe it's just an indication, and the lockers aren't on."

But when I try some turns, the differential lockers are definitely engaged, as evidenced by the extra effort needed to steer the quad. There's no way Margy can ride all day in this condition. Plus, whatever is wrong could do damage to her bike.

We check the owner's manual, but it's typical of most equipment manuals these days – poorly written, with few details to aid in the solution of operational problems. There's no troubleshooting information, and it's not even clear how to operate the lockers switch, although I think we're doing everything right.

"Let me drive it a bit, and maybe it'll go away," says Margy, so I relinquish her bike, not confident the problem will simply go away.

But it does! After driving her quad through another series of turns, there's an audible *clunk*, as the lockers disengage. We seldom use our differential lockers, and probably her engagement system has atrophied from lack of use. Mechanical systems sometimes act that way.

I'm elated! What looked like an aborted ride after our first barge off-load is now back on again. Off we go!

Departing the staging area, we face an immediate decision as the road splits at a "Y." I select the route to the left, which leads down to the log dump area, not where I'd intended to go. Certainly, we're not lost so soon, but it's a notably awkward start.

Back on Clover Main, we climb through beautiful thick groves of evergreens. We ascend gently, which is ideal terrain for Margy, with picturesque Clover Lake to our left. At the Intersection with Frogpond South, we exit Clover Main, and start the more intense climb into the stands of older trees. We stop at a turnout, where we look down on Clover Lake, with Powell Lake in the background.

Looking down on Clover Lake

Today's ride is long by our standards, and we don't stop again until we've passed Frogpond and its outlet that drops dramatically down into Powell Lake. There's more to explore, but it can wait until another time. There will be lots of trips like this to barge ramps all along Powell Lake – a huge dream now coming true.

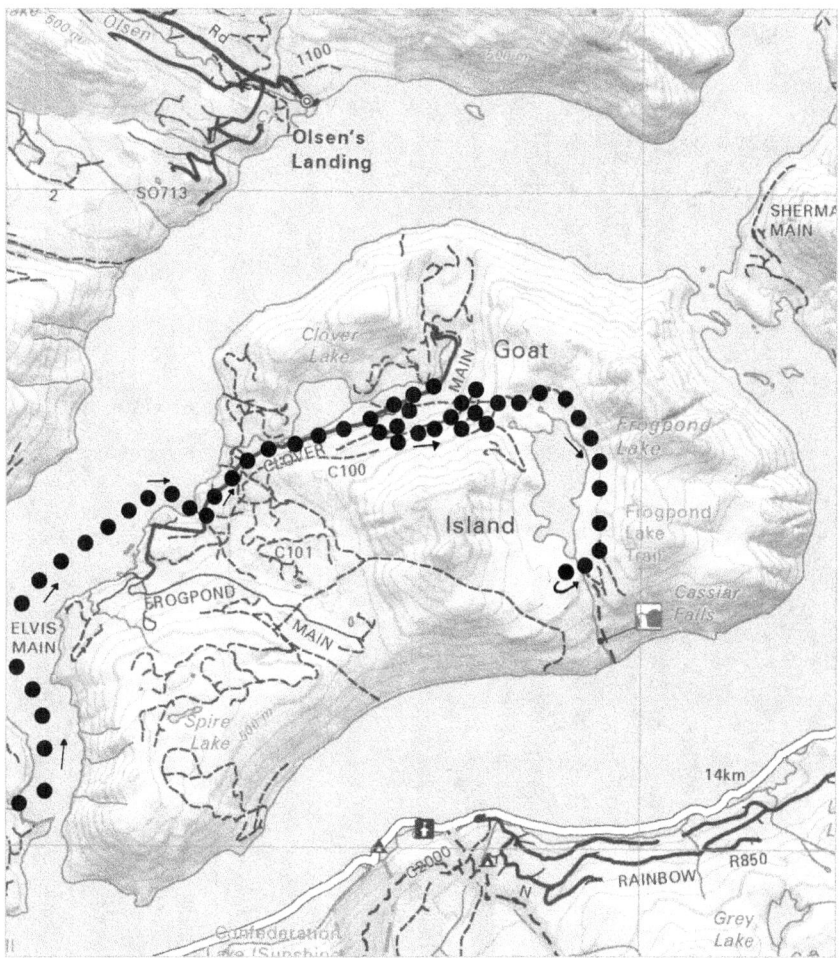

Goat Lake Trip

At the end of our ride, the on-load of our quads goes flawlessly. This time, when I pull the last metal ramp from the shore, I'm ready for any drift that may occur. Without delay, I push off. Margy quickly lowers and starts the engine, and we're on our way.

Once we exit the area of the log boom, I step back onto the swim-grid, and start the 9.9-horsepower kicker. Then I shut off the 50-horse outboard, and we settle into a slow troll home, fishing for trout. We slide past Elvis Point at about 3 klicks, slow enough to catch a fish if any are around today. But it doesn't matter whether we catch one or not. We're on our barge, and joyous just to be here.

Chapter 12

Narrows

Narrows Main Dock, Powell Lake BC

A FEW DAYS AFTER OUR FIRST BARGE TRIP to Goat Island, Margy and I depart Hole in the Wall mid-day for our first overnight trip on the barge. The weather forecast is for cloudy skies, and even a prospect of showers in the afternoon, but then clearing overnight. The possibility of rain doesn't daunt us in the least. We're used to adverse conditions in a tent, and prone to making adventure out of whatever comes along.

As we exit the Hole, I drive while Margy rides up front, sitting on her quad near the bow. Our destination is what Rudi calls Narrows,

Departing Hole in the Wall

an inactive logging area on the east end of Powell Lake near where it joins Goat River. At barge speed, we expect to be travelling for about two hours.

As we motor along the south side of Goat Island, I focus my binoculars on the far shore, where Doug is rebuilding an old land cabin. So far, his biggest achievement has been a small dock and a palatial outhouse. He often starts small on projects that tend to grow to immense proportions.

"Doug's there!" I yell excitedly to Margy.

In the binoculars, I can see a boat at Doug's dock, a nearly sure sign that Doug is working on his cabin (or maybe another enhancement to the outhouse). Of course, he might be simply lounging on the deck or swimming. Doug's a big-time swimmer, covering more klicks on an average swim than anyone else I know.

It takes another twenty minutes to cover the distance across the lake to Doug's cabin. As the view grows in my binoculars, I can now see two people on the dock, probably Doug and his brother, Malcolm, who I call the "Crazy New Zealanders." They may not be totally crazy, but they sure are a lot of fun.

As we get closer, I notice that the boat at the dock is the one Doug bought in Seattle. He and I brought it back on a trailer to Bellingham, and then Doug towed it the rest of the way to Powell River by himself. It has since been totally refurbished, something Doug does regularly to old boats.

Yes, it's the two brothers on the dock, and they're glad to see our barge up close. Doug and I have talked about this boat for months. In fact, he's the one who first pointed out to me that it was for sale. Once I saw it, I couldn't stop until I owned it.

Doug and Malcolm greet us at the dock, where they make an exuberant inspection of our deck arrangement and cab. Margy and I act like proud parents, as we point out the fine features of the barge that are immediately appreciated by avid boaters like these two.

"Go check out the outhouse," says Doug. "It's finally finished. Now if only I could make this old cabin look half as good."

Margy and I trek the short path to the outhouse, which hasn't been over-advertised as "palatial." It's both huge and resplendent. I've never seen a finer outhouse.

Doug and Malcomb

Leaving Doug's cabin, we remain on the south side of the lake, which allows us to check out the logging dock and ramp at Fiddlehead near the old "Farm." This will be one of our main entry points to the

Doug's palatial outhouse

vast trail network used by the Powell River ATV Club on a regular basis. We look forward to revisiting these roads and trails, and meeting friends who we haven't ridden with for years.

Past Fiddlehead, we continue along the lake's south shore, looking for the wine-coloured cabin we almost bought over a decade ago, when we first became enchanted with the concept of a floating home. It's easily identified on the shore, still purplish in colour and looking much the same as it did on our first visit fourteen years ago. Life would have been so different if we'd purchased this cabin. In fact, it seems possible circumstances would have led us in a completely different direction. There would have been no John in our life, and what a difference that would have made! Would we still be here on this lake? Would we be coming here only as a vacation getaway? Even small deviations in life's path can multiply to major changes that will never be known. Seeing the wine-coloured cabin always reminds me of what might have been, and it's not the splendid oneness with the environment we've found at Hole in the Wall. I'm eternally grateful for what we have in our floating life on Powell Lake.

The spit of land to our left, angling down from the northeast, marks the place called "Narrows." Rudi has told us about the two barge ramps, mentioning the less distinctive "No Name" landing beyond Goat River to the east, farther up into Goat Lake. On our map, the log dump is shown behind the main promontory north of the Narrows landing. Years ago, John and I docked around the headland on the south side and explored with our small off-road motorcycles (*Up the Main*, Chapter 20).

To get an overview of the dock and ramp, we swing past the spot we used with the motorcycles. It's an ideal place to off-load our quads and tie up for the night. Then we motor back west along the shore, rounding the peninsula towards the other "Narrows" shown on our logging map, which may be only the log dump.

As we head north along the small peninsula, we pass the only currently-occupied cabin in the area, located scenically on the point. This is a Sunday in early June, so we expect more activity in this area, but so far this year things have been rather quiet on Powell Lake. On the other hand, the sky is cloudy and the forecast is for rain later today, so maybe most people have already gone back to town.

The log booming area we find on the far side of the headlands is large but inactive. Now we understand some of our "Narrows" confusion. There's no dock here, just the log dump. On the other side of the promontory, only a short distance by road, lies the logging dock and barge ramp. The entire complex is called Narrows, although these two spots are separated by a greater distance when travelled by boat. We reverse course, and return to the dock and ramp to off-load our quads.

This time, I carefully watch the depth-sounder as we approach the shore, and it remains well within a comfortable range, never dropping below 6 feet even when we contact the shore with the bow. So I keep the motor idling and tilted nearly full-down while we off-load our bikes.

Narrows Barge Ramp

When the barge's rolling stock is on shore, I push off from the bow, while Margy backs the boat towards the nearby dock. We quickly tie up for the night, pitching our tent on the deck of the barge. While pulling into Narrows, we had experienced a few intermittent sprinkles. Now, only a few minutes after setting up our tent, it begins to rain. Just in time!

Tent on barge

The next 3 hours are spent lounging and reading in the tent, waiting for the rain to stop. It's a relaxing time, although an afternoon slated for riding is slipping away. Finally, blue sky peeks through the tent's door, as the sun drops towards the horizon. Still, with the long days of June, we have plenty of time to explore.

It takes only a few minutes to prepare for our ride. I start my engine first, and drive up the steep incline leading out of the dock area. I stop at the top of the first hill, waiting for Margy.

After sitting on my quad for a while, watching for Margy's bike in my rearview mirror, I begin to wonder what's delaying her. Things seem to be going slower than normal for the beginning of a simple ride.

A few minutes later, when I glace in my mirror again, there's Margy, but she's walking towards me rather than riding. I get off my quad and walk back to meet her.

"I'm out of fuel," she says.

"No way!" I reply. "Both of our tanks are full."

At least, I think they're full. After our last ride on Goat Island, I refilled both quads, along with the barge's fuel tank. I specifically remember refilling the barge tank from a gas can, marveling at how little fuel we burned on that trip. Then again, I don't specifically recall refueling our quads.

We walk back to my bike, and I check it's fuel gauge. It hovers on empty. Oh, we're both out of fuel, aren't we? How could this have happened? Now I remember the sequence of things. We left our old parking area near Hole in the Wall for the first barge on-load at Chippewa Bay with full tanks. But the ride was so short I didn't refuel our bikes after the short ride. Then we barged to Goat Island, and I refueled the boat when we returned home. I failed to put gas in the quads, and here we are without fuel in our tanks. My barge checklist has let me down. I make a mental note to add the obvious, "gas for quads," to the list.

However, all isn't lost, since we have lots of spare fuel, including a container we carry on the back of Margy's quad and a can aboard the barge. Using Margy's spare gas, I nearly fill both quads. Plus, we're not really empty, since the "Reserve" lever on our bikes provides 20 additional klicks of travel. Still, it was a silly situation, although easily resolved, and an important lesson for the future.

We begin our ride with a short trip across the peninsula to the log dump, where the bay looks north towards Rainbow Lodge. We'll travel there someday soon to ride Shermans Main in an area we've never explored.

From the Narrows log dump we ride along the scenic main that parallels the shoreline along Goat River and Goat Lake. But a short distance past the turnoff to Narrows North, the road abruptly ends, with big cut logs purposefully crossing the main, warning of what's ahead. I get off my bike and walk to the spot where a small creek meanders through a deep gully. The bridge has been washed away or intentionally removed, and we can travel no farther. By my estimation

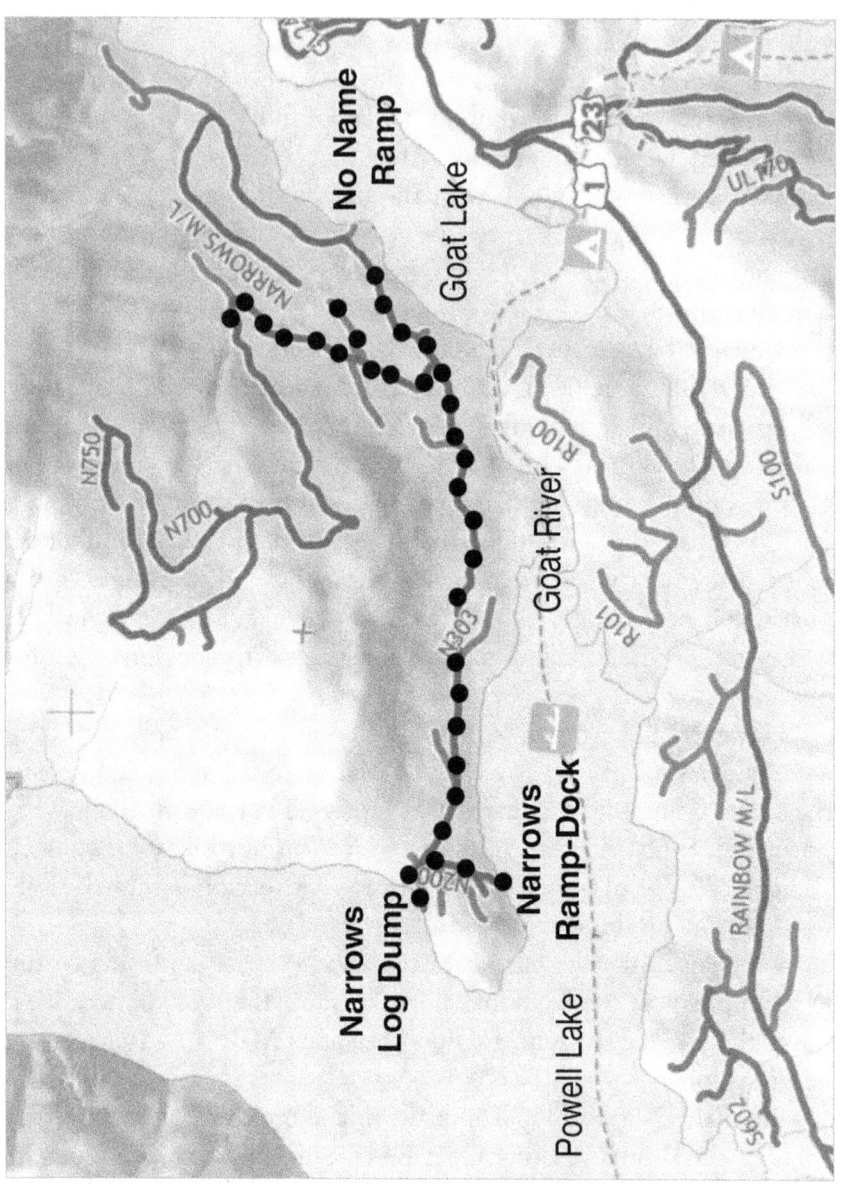

(and a glance at the GPS), we're within a klick of what I think is "No Name," as described by Rudi. This break cuts off the rest of Narrows Main and its associated logging spurs, but on a future trip, we should be able to barge to "No Name," and rejoin the mainline there.

We turn around and head back to the junction, turning uphill on Narrows North, climbing quickly in terrain that begins to disturb Margy. I can tell she's affected by the incline, as she gradually slows. Finally, she pulls over to the side of the road, and signals that it's time to turn around. The majestic turnoff where we're stopped looks down on Goat Lake, shrouded in patchy clouds below.

Looking down on Goat Lake

There's no concern with reversing course, since this has been enough riding for today. We'll have more opportunities tomorrow. There's still plenty of light, but it's getting darker, an added incentive to head back to the dock.

Returning to Narrows Dock

Back on Narrows Main, we ride west, into the setting sun. The contrasts in colour and definition in the forest this time of day are always spectacular. Strong hues of dark and light spread before us. I call it "increased resolution," like comparing an old computer monitor to a brand new model.

When we're within a klick of the logging dock, a strange situation presents itself. Afterwards, it seems perfectly obvious what was happening, but at the time it's somewhat of a mystery.

Suddenly, in the middle of the road, a family of geese appear – mom and dad along with four goslings too small to fly. At first, this seems like something we see often, but then I realize we're a long ways from the water. Horizontally, the bay where the logging dock sits is less than a klick away, but the vertical distance above the water is at least 100 metres. That's quite a climb for these non-flying babies. It's not a vertical face, but it must have been a very steep clamber. Why would a family including non-fledged geese be walking way up here?

The other mystery is why they remain on the road when they see our quads. The parents are obviously upset, turning and honking at Margy and me, while the entire family continues clumsily down the road in front of us. The goslings are obviously in distress, too, running from side to side while they're herded by mom. Meanwhile, dad is the most upset of all, dropping behind the rest of the family and spitting at us. So we stop.

"Let's give them a chance to get off the road," I say to Margy. "Seems weird to find them this far from the water. Why would they come up here?"

"Not sure," replies Margy. "Their nests are usually near the shore. Must have been a big climb for the kids."

"They're out of sight now," I say. "Probably off the road by now. Let's go."

When we round the next bend, the geese are still on the road, walking downhill towards the dock still a long ways in front of them. They are again agitated by our presence. Maybe if we try to pass, they'll get off the road, and we'll be out of their way.

I rev up my engine, which results in scaring mom and babies off the main, which seems like a good thing. But dad takes an aggressive stand in the middle of the road. Then the big goose flutters ahead of us, down the road. Later we decide he's doing the logical fatherly thing, leading us away from the rest of the family as a defensive tactic. For another half-klick, we follow him, as he flies forward in short bursts, doing his job of protecting his family. But now he's a long way from mom and the babies, so I'm concerned about him finding them again. Finally, he hops off the road, barely in the bushes, and we pass slowly as he spits some more. He cranes his long neck towards us, and gives us a final hiss.

Once we're back at the dock, I ask Margy if she's worried about dad finding the rest of his family.

"Don't think so," she replies. "He knew what he was doing, and he did his job well. I heard him honking as we pulled away, probably already sending a hero's message to the rest of the brood."

As we sit in our lawn chairs on the dock, discussing the geese some more, we hear a nearby honk.

"There they are!" says Margy.

Two full-grown geese and four chicks glide past the dock, near enough to reach. Now that they're back in the water, they aren't afraid of us – floating by slowly, content and undaunted. Nature takes care of itself, if we leave it alone.

Camping on the barge

Chapter 13

Olsen's

Olsen's Landing, Theodosia River

THE CONCEPT OF USING THE LOGGING DOCKS of Powell Lake as a jumping off point for exploration of remote backcountry has come nearly full circle. When this book began, John and I found ourselves motoring north to the Head, pushing our quads on a raft. Our mode of transportation may have been rustic, but it closely matched the more elaborate capabilities of our new barge. So far, Margy and I have tackled several logging ramps on the lake, expanding our stay from a day-trip to an overnight journey. It's obvious we're almost back to where we began, with a major trip to the Head in the near future.

First, however, we need at least one more local overnighter to work out a few remaining kinks. Besides, this book is almost full – more to the point, it's as big as it can get and still allow economic publication. So it would be nice to end this book with a final shakedown cruise. At my cabin, I put together a map of current and future trips. The diagram shows the location of the barge ramps on Powell Lake, places I've been or plan to go in this and future books.

We consider this our final test journey, ironing out the wrinkles in taking the barge to shore and camping on the deck. Chip North is our first consideration, but riding there is limited. So instead we plan to visit Olsen's Landing, one of our perennial favourites, although never previously an overnight destination. We've often stopped here while cruising in a boat, walking up Olsen's Main for a quick trek into the forest. And Margy, John, and I have even ridden our quads here from Theodosia Valley, a long day on the trails.

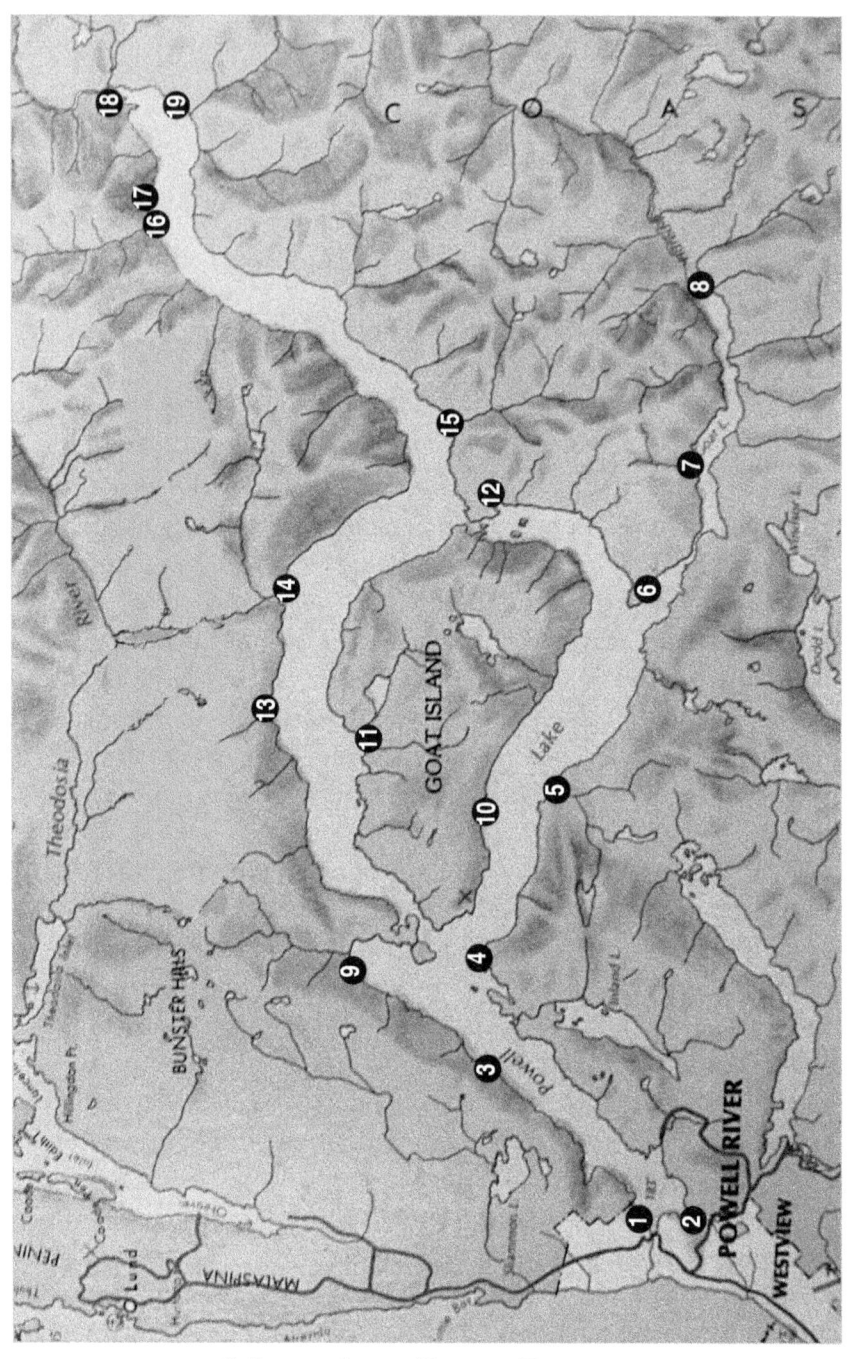

Map – Area Barge Ramps

Barge Ramps
Powell Lake & Goat Lake

1 – Shinglemill

2 – Mowat Bay

3 – Chipp South

4 – Pickle Point

5 – Fiddlehead Farm

6 – Narrows

7 – No Name (Narrows)

8 – No Name (Public Ramp)

9 – Chippewa Bay

10 – Dunn (Goat Island)

11 – Goat Island (Clover Main)

12 – Shermans (Rainbow Lodge)

13 – Chipp North

14 – Olsen's Landing

15 – Beartooth

16 – Billy Goat

17 – No Name (Billy Goat North)

18 – The Head (Daniels Main)

19 – Inactive (Jim Brown)

Legend – Area Barge Ramps

We motor out of Hole in the Wall in the barge, traveling along Goat Island, past float cabins still unoccupied in mid-June. We travel near shore, enjoying a close look at the cabins we know so well. Rounding Elvis Point, still cruising close-in, a yellow-and-black tug appears right off our bow. It's not dangerously close, but we need to change course right away to miss the tug and its towed cargo, road building equipment probably coming from the nearby Goat Island ramp we still call Clover Dock. Or maybe this vessel is returning from Shermans Main near Rainbow Lodge, farther north, where logging activity is currently underway. In both cases, Elvis Point sits along the shortest route south to Block Bay where logging equipment is mustered. I flick my bright spotlights on-and-off so the tug driver knows I see him. He's hard to miss, of course, but it always helps when the other guy knows you're not asleep.

Farther north, we cross over from the Goat Island side of the lake to the western shore, headed directly towards Olsen's Landing. The water, as is typical for this portion of the lake, is choppy, but well within the capabilities of our barge.

"There's a boat at the resort," says Margy, referring to Powell River Resort and it's small cabins on the bluff.

"Probably the *Mugwump*," I reply. "I haven't seen it at the Shinglemill for months."

The *Mugwump* usually sits on the public dock at the Shinglemill, moored there for at least a decade. The unusual almost-a-houseboat with its old diesel engine has been advertised as part of the deal for anyone interested in purchasing Powell River Resort, a real estate offering that's been listed for the past few years. The resort seems like such a good idea, from a commercial standpoint, but similar enterprising ideas on the lake haven't gone anywhere. One of the problems is the lack of road access. The *Mugwump* is supposed to solve that problem.

"Nothing going on," says Margy. "The cabins look vacant, but in pretty good shape."

At one time, during one of my many bouts of insanity, I seriously considered buying the *Mugwump* as a vessel to cruise the chuck, when it was being offered separately from the resort. Fortunately, John talked me out of it. Otherwise, I'd still be trying unsuccessfully to make it sea-worthy for the ocean. That's just what I need on the chuck – an old diesel and a vessel not designed for big waves.

Approaching Olsen's Landing, Beartooth to the north sports its own cap-cloud, a single cumulus in an otherwise deep blue sky. Beyond Olsen's Landing, Dalgleish Valley cuts upward into the high country, splitting off from Olsen's Main in a steep rise. I remember being there with John many years ago, during one of my visits to Olsen's Landing from Theodosia. Beautiful vistas overlook Powell Lake from Dalgleish, or at least they did before the road began to deteriorate after it's last use for active logging. Maybe we can ride the lower portion of the old road today. The upper part is undoubtedly clogged with alders.

As we pull in towards Olsen's barge ramp, a crosswind blows in from our left, with waves bigger than we've experienced before when beaching this barge. Margy stands ready with a pike pole near the stern, prepared to steady the boat from swinging until I can get the metal ramps connected to shore. We know the ramps have a stabilizing influence, and they should prove adequate again today. But until I deploy them, it's a big unknown.

In this crosswind condition, I decide to execute our arrival by allowing the barge to drift towards shore at a slow pace, while shutting off the engine and raising the leg to avoid contacting the prop with the upsloping beach. I worry about underwater rocks we may be blown against on the downwind side. It's a technique that works in calm conditions, but proves difficult to manage today.

As soon as the bow touches bottom, the stern begins to swing. Margy is able to counteract it with the pike pole, but we'll learn there's a better way that makes for easier landings. On future more-successful arrivals in a crosswind, I'll maintain forward power on the engine to solid contact with the beach after we land.

My initial fears of becoming grounded by too firm a landing have repeatedly proven pointless. The 50-horsepower engine works fine at backing us off the beach, even in a partially trimmed-up position, and solid contact at the barge ramp provides for controlled off-loads. We admit to being novices, but we're learning.

Our quads are on shore in just a few minutes. Then I jostle the metal ramps back onto the barge, push on the bow (without engine power today), and we successfully slip back away from shore. Meanwhile,

Margy keeps the boat straight with the pike pole until we're in deep enough water to feel comfortable starting the engine. All in all, our barge has been easier to deal with than I expected. With our ever-increasing experience, it gets even easier over time.

We motor over to the dock, tie up, set up our tent, and get ready to ride.

Olsen's Landing

Within an hour, we're climbing up Olsen's Main. In the first klick of travel, a bear appears, running up the road, obviously not wanting anything to do with us. He (or she) is a full-grown animal, using the logging road as an easy path to its destination, interrupted today by humans on quads. We stop immediately, and after the bear disappears around the bend, we wait a few minutes more, and then ease our way up the road until its apparent the animal is well out of sight.

I think about my can of bear spray behind me in my quad's aft box. Little good it does me there, but I decide to proceed for now, stopping soon to retrieve the container of spray. Simultaneously, I realize I've left my GPS back at the boat, although the roads here are pretty straightforward. In other words, I've started this ride without the attention to details that I should have given it. But it's a beautiful day, and nature – even the bear – is obviously at peace with these imposing humans.

The first major road to the right looks properly placed to be Dagleish Main, although there's no sign (and no GPS). We turn onto it, and begin to climb.

The old main is in pretty good shape, not deactivated by large trenches or overgrown from the sides, as is so often the case for inactive logging roads. As we proceed upward, I notice landmarks that ring a faint bell, even a spot looking a lot like the vista where Margy took a photo on our last visit, when we stopped to ponder the beauty of Powell Lake below. It's one of my favourite pictures of John, Bro, and me, which I call "Two Guys and a Dog," Today, this picturesque spot (or what I think is the same spot) is so completely overgrown that it would be a major slog through berry bushes to get to the now bush-covered slope where John, Bro, and I sat and pondered the lake years ago (*Farther Up the Main*, Chapter 10).

Two Guys and a Dog

Margy leads for most of the climb, and she advances upward at a pace faster than I would expect, considering the drop-off to the side. But because thick bushes line the edge of the road, she rides in confidence. Without the vegetation, she would probably slow to a crawl or even stop, but today we continue upwards quite a few kliks before the path becomes severely overgrown and difficult to navigate.

"I'll take a look ahead," I suggest, as I pull up beside her, nodding towards the canopied road in front of us. "I'm surprised we made it this far. Is this a good place for you to wait for me?"

"Sure," she replies.

Margy is good about relaxing while I go ahead in situations like this. In this case, we've stopped at a wide-open section of the road, with easy turnarounds on both sides. I figure I'll be able to ride only a little farther before the road will be completely blocked by alders.

Surprisingly, the old main doesn't become overgrown for quite a ways, so I continue upward. But in another klik, I notice high cliffs lining the uphill side of my path, which looks like a perfect spot for a mountain lion – exactly the reason I bought a can of bear spray in the first place. After John, Bro, and I encountered a cougar that seemed to be in a dog-eating mood near Heather Main (*Off the Grid*, Chapter 17), I realized I needed to travel with a can of bear spray at the ready. I'm not sure how effective it would be on a cougar, but I do know thoughts of mountain lions are a lot more troublesome to me than worries about bears.

I finally stop, and retrieve the can of spray from my aft compartment. Now I'll ride with the container on a strap draped around my neck. I still don't have my GPS, of course, and now I realize I should have brought our walkie-talkies along today. They are a great help in situations like this, to let Margy know where I am and when I'll be back. In fact, if had the walkie-talkies, I'd probably suggest she drive up the main to join me, since the road has still not become completely impassable.

But without a way to communicate, I decide to ride only a little farther uphill before turning around. The main is in much better shape than I'd expected, but I finally reverse course when I approach a major trench. I'm sure I could get across it in my quad, but it's best to tackle spots like this with two sets of eyes rather than one. As I maneuver my bike in the course reversal, this spot jogs my memory. I'm pretty sure it's where John decided to spend some time gathering big rocks and partially filling the trench for the safety of those who would use this route in the future.

Once I rejoin Margy below, we head down Dagleish, and out onto Olsen's Main. We barely start up the road when a big elk appears around the bend. This is a Roosevelt Elk, one of the species relocated here from the lower mainland. They've thrived in this environment, usually seen in herds rather than individually. This one looks like a big doe (no visible horns), travelling by herself, but not willing to get off the road to let us pass. She stops for a moment, looks back at us, and then jogs slowly up the road. We give her plenty of time to disappear, but she stops again, looks back, and then slowly trots out of sight around the next curve. We provide this beautiful creature plenty of time to get away from humans, and then resume our trip up the main.

(We experience another elk sighting later in the day, on our way back down Olsen's Main, but my guess is it's the same animal.)

Today, early in our trip, we've seen more wildlife (a bear and an elk) than we've seen on any of our rides in the past few years. John reports (after we return to our cabin) that on this same day in Theodosia Valley he saw six bears.

The next major offshoot to our right is an old road exiting the main just before we reach the top of Olsen's Lake. (The lake remains invisible on our left.) There's a severely-faded sign at the intersection, so I ride up close to it and stop. It's hard to read, but pale red letters on a white background seem to say: *Hell.*

Margy comes over to the sign, and stops beside me. She shrugs, and I don't say anything, but I'm pretty sure neither of us is certain what the sign says. I look at it again more closely. It's barely readable, but this really might be the highly touted road to Hell. Of course, if I had my GPS today, I would know for sure.

We start up the road, overgrown like Dalgleish Main, but easily navigable. It never becomes fully canopied to the point where our

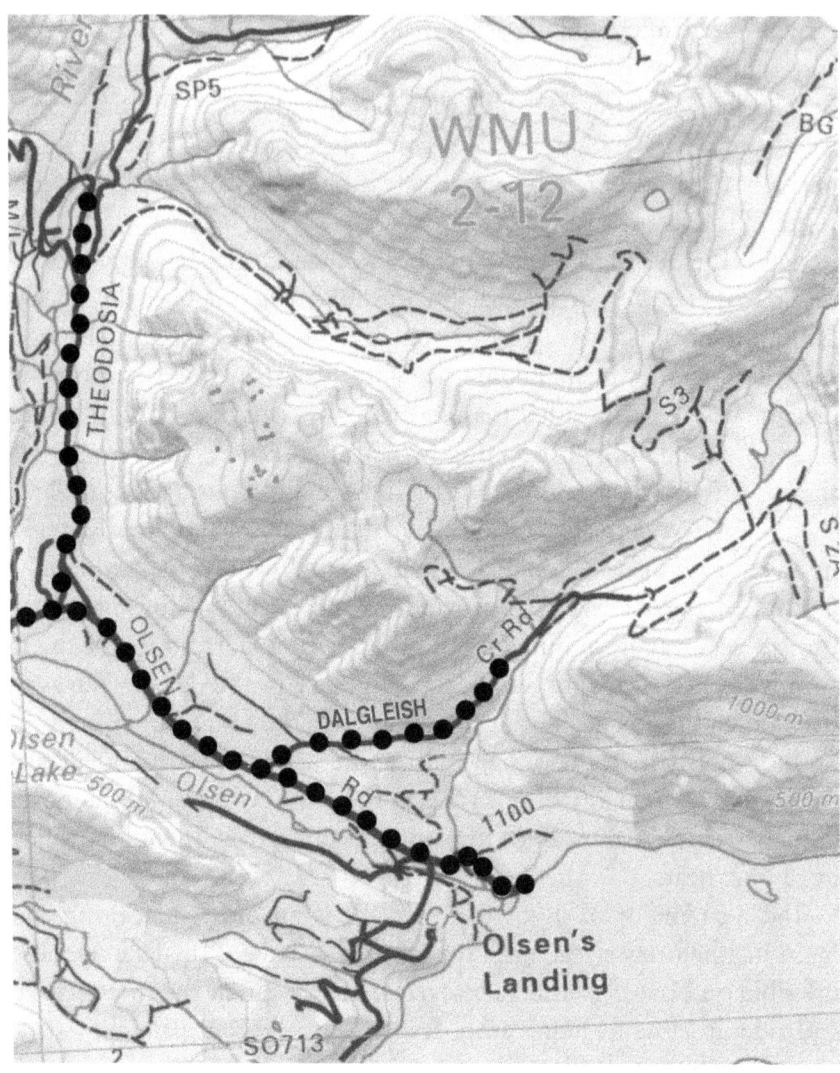

progress is stopped. Margy leads, as we climb through some initially formidable-looking sections where I expect her to stop. But then the old main opens a bit, and we keep climbing. Margy slows at several spots to push aside the intruding branches or breaks them off. If more work is needed, I follow her through, stopping briefly to use my big pruning shears to cut the branches to make our return trip easier.

We continue to climb, klick after klick, in an area where big trees and dense forest thrust up on both sides. In one spot, we stop and marvel at an old logging slash, where the huge stumps look at least a hundred years old. It's a grove of fallen old growth rivaling any slash I've ever seen.

We stop to examine an old flatbed logging truck that has pulled (or been pushed) off the road. The vehicle is now almost entirely overgrown with vegetation. The forest has reclaimed it, seemingly after many years. But the truck is actually in pretty good condition, and there's even air left in the tires. The side door says: *Manor Holdings, Coquitlam BC, Canada.*

Abandoned truck near Theodosia River

"I wonder how long it takes for all the air to leak out of tires?" asks Margy.

"I'm thinking exactly the same thing. This truck may have been here for decades, or maybe only a few years."

We continue uphill, crossing a still-solid bridge over a big stream that barrels downhill from our right. Its cascading falls provide an impressive cut through the surrounding forest. I pull up behind Margy, and shut off my engine.

"The road to hell is paved with good intensions," I say.

Margy looks at me oddly, like she has no idea what I'm referring to.

"You saw the sign didn't you?" I ask.

"This must be the falls," she says. "That's what the sign said."

"You mean you think the sign said *Falls*? I thought the sign said *Hell*."

She gives me another odd look, but laughs. Usually, when there's a difference between what she sees and what I see, she's almost always right. So the sign must have been telling us about these falls.

"A lot prettier than Hell," I joke.

A little farther up the old main, there's another falls. This one is much more impressive, although the bridge we stop on is badly

Creek into Theososia River

deteriorated on one side. Someone has laid pink tape along the edge as a caution to drive on the more-solid flank.

Continuing farther uphill, the main is starting to close in. But off to our left, barely visible through the thick bushes, is a deep ravine. Now I get it! – this is the road paralleling Theodosia River, following it up towards its high source in the mountains. I've been here before, too, also with John. Now I'm looking through the trees at an amazing waterfall. During one of my first quad rides into Theodosia Valley, we continued on Theodosia Main to the turnoff we took today. Then we climbed on this road (still designated as Theodosia Main) where it jogs dramatically upward. We stopped beside this big waterfall plunging down the mountain.

Below us, just above Olsen's Lake, the flow splits, with most of the water continuing down to the sea, and part of the stream pouring first into Olsen's Lake and then down to Powell Lake. Long ago, most of the water was artificially diverted into Olsen's Lake, to allow it to reach the power-hungry dam at the south end of Powell Lake. In recent years, the man-made diversion sends more water into the lower Theodosia River, where a rejuvenated salmon spawning stream has prospered.

We decide not to climb any higher. This is the pinnacle of a beautiful ride. From here, we head slowly back down Theodosia Main, pass the two smaller waterfalls, the abandoned logging truck beside the road, and the huge old growth stumps in the slash. When we finally reach the junction with Olsen's Main, I pull up to the faded sign to read it again. I expect it to say *Falls*, now that I know what to anticipate. But no, it definitely says *Hell*, somebody's idea of a severe contradiction in life.

We ride the short distance to Olsen's Lake, where we gaze at the remaining flow of Theodosia water diverted under the bridge. I fish the stream, while Margy rides her quad through the quarry with its connecting trail to the lake's shore. I don't catch any fish, and Margy doesn't stay very long at the beach, and then we're on our way again.

It's a short downhill ride back to Olsen's Landing and our barge. When the dock pops into view, our tent and temporary lakeside home await us. Another quad ride, followed by a relaxing evening, sitting in camping chairs on another logging dock. And another night in our cozy tent, dreaming of even more adventures on Powell Lake.

Olsen's Landing campsite

Geographic Index

Blue Ridge   p.95
Blue Trail   p.70
Bunster Range   p.127-131
Chippewa Bay   p.12-13, 19, 96, 98, 100, 102, 107, 109-110, 114-116, 122, 127-128, 130, 131-132, 135-137, 149-153, 158-159, 169, 177
Clover Main/Dock (Goat Island)   p.20-21, 156, 160, 177, 178
Cypress Main   p.35, 37, 49, 51-52, 55-57, 50-60
Dagleish Main   p.181, 183
Daniels Main/River   p.37-43, 60, 177
Dunn Main/Dock   p.177.
Duck Lake   p.70, 74, 80-81, 88-92
Edgehill Trail/School   p.70-72, 80, 88-91, 93
Eldred River   p.50
Elk lake   p.80, 87-88, 93-95
Elvis Point   p.162, 178
Fiddlehead Farm/Dock   p.13, 165-166, 177
Frogpond (Goat Island)   p.160
Giovanno Main/Lake   p.70, 76-77
Goat Lake   p.13, 19, 50, 132, 161, 166, 169, 171, 177
Goat Main   p.13
Granite Lake   p.80-81, 92-93
Haslam Main/Lake   p.70, 74-75, 77
Head of Powell Lake   p.13, 15, 18-21, 27-28, 30-35, 37, 41, 46-50, 53, 56-58, 61-62, 66, 137, 175, 177
Heather Main   p.67-69, 97-100, 102-103, 107, 110-111, 115, 123, 132, 182
Hole in the Wall (Powell Lake)   p.12-15, 17, 19-21, 23-25, 28, 63, 69, 81, 99-100, 102, 104, 108, 110-111, 117, 122-123, 127, 132, 148-149, 154, 156, 159, 163, 166, 169, 175
Jim Brown Main/Creek   p.47, 49, 51, 177
Last Chance Trail   p.82, 102-105

Geographic Index

Mud Lake   p.92
Museum Main   p.12, 96, 132, 135-136
Narrows Main/Dock   p.166-169, 171-172, 177
No Name Ramp (Narrows)   p.166, 171, 177
Olsen's Landing/Main   p.12, 20-21, 97, 132, 175, 177-180, 183, 187, 188
Powell Main   p.38, 42-43
Saltery Bay   p.133-134, 140-141, 145-146
Shinglemill (Powell Lake)   p.15-16, 18-19, 21-25, 63, 100, 103-104, 122, 128-129, 133, 145, 147-148, 177-178
Sliammon Lake   p.129
Southview Road   p.83, 85, 100, 104, 129
Theodosia Valley   p.12, 63, 65, 80-82, 84, 85-87, 100-101, 104, 106-107, 110, 122, 132, 175, 179, 183, 185, 187
Toba Inlet   p.39, 40

About the Author

From 1980 to 2005, Wayne Lutz was Chairman of the Aeronautics Department at Mount San Antonio College in Los Angeles. He also served 20 years as a U.S. Air Force C-130 aircraft maintenance officer. His educational background includes a B.S. degree in physics from the University of Buffalo and an M.S. in systems management from the University of Southern California. The author is a flight instructor with 7000 hours of flying experience.

The author resides in a floating cabin on Canada's Powell Lake in all seasons, and occasionally in a city-folk condo in Bellingham, Washington. His writing genres include regional Canadian publications and science fiction. This is his third book regarding off-road riding in coastal British Columbia. Contact the author at wlutz@mtsac.edu

Author interviewing Bro on his quad in Theodosia Valley

Coastal British Columbia Stories

by Wayne J. Lutz

Up the Lake
Up the Main
Up the Winter Trail
Up the Strait
Up the Airway
Farther Up the Lake
Farther Up the Main
Farther Up the Strait
Cabin Number 5
Off the Grid
Up the Inlet
Beyond the Main

Future Titles:
Powell Lake by Barge and Quad
Islands and Inlets

Other Books by Wayne J. Lutz

Science Fiction Titles

Echo of a Distant Planet
Inbound to Earth
Across the Gallactic Sea
Anomaly at Fortune Lake
When Galaxies Collide

Pacific Northwest Series

Paddling the Pacific Northwest
Flying the Pacific Northwest

Beyond the Main is the 12th in a series of volumes focusing on the unique places and memorable people of coastal British Columbia

Order at:
www.PowellRiverBooks.com

Coastal BC Living Blog
PowellRiverBooks.blogspot.com

www.ingramcontent.com/pod-product-compliance
Lightning Source LLC
Chambersburg PA
CBHW071732080526
44588CB00013B/2002